Joseph Grim Feinberg

PRAISE BOSS!

The Erotic Adventures of Mr. Block

CHARLES H. KERR
PUBLISHING COMPANY

ISBN: 978-0-88286-009-1
Library of Congress cataloging in publication: 2022934178

Cover linocut and lettering by Vlocke,
with additional illustrations by Ernest Riebe
Design and typesetting by J. Dakota Brown
Typefaces: Garamond Premier Pro, Cooper Black, Bernard MT

Printed in the U.S. on acid-free paper.

Charles H. Kerr Publishing Company
8901 S. Exchange Ave.
Chicago, IL 60617
www.charleshkerr.com

Or,

Labor's Loves Lost

A Proletarian Sex Tragicomedy in Five Acts

CHARLES H. KERR
PUBLISHING COMPANY

Introduction

"[Mr. Block] is representative of that host of slaves who think in terms of their masters. Mr. Block owns nothing, yet he speaks from the standpoint of the millionaire; he is patriotic without patrimony; he is a law-abiding outlaw ... [who] licks the hand that smites him and kisses the boot that kicks him ... the personification of all that a worker should not be."[1]

Walker C. Smith,
editor of the *Industrial Worker*, 1913

This description of Mr. Block, a newspaper comic strip anti-hero, appeared in the introduction to a pamphlet that reprinted 24 of his adventures in 1913. Drawn by Ernest Riebe, a German immigrant, Mr. Block first appeared in the Industrial Workers of the World's (IWW or Wobblies) newspaper the *Industrial Worker* in 1912. The IWW, founded in Chicago in 1905, were (and still are) an international labor union that aimed to organize everyone in a workplace irrespective of rank or job role. A grassroots organization, they rejected centralized leadership and preached a blend of syndicalism, anarchism,

1. Walker C. Smith, "Introductory," in *Twenty-four Cartoons of Mr. Block*, ed. Ernest Riebe (Chicago: Charles H. Kerr Publishing Company, 1984).

and communism. Their methods were egalitarian. They published newspapers written by and for workers containing contributions from members around the country, including cartoons, as well as articles by famous socialists such as Jack London and IWW founder members: Emma Goldman, "Mother" Jones, "Big Bill" Haywood, and Eugene Debs.

The IWW were particularly famous for their "Little Red Song Book" where the majority of the songs (in the 1913 edition) were written by the Swedish Wobbly Joe Hill. These were sung on strikes, at demonstrations, and while working. Hill's song "Mister Block," based on the comic strip, achieved long lasting and international acclaim and was heard at meetings and picket lines, including in 1913 in California when the sheriff and his deputies fired on striking hop-pickers as they sang. Hill's chorus aptly sums up the character of Mr. Block:

> His head is made of lumber and solid as a rock;
> he is a common worker
> And his name is Mr. Block.
> And Block thinks he may
> Be President some day[2]

Mr Block's head was simply a lump of wood. He was a "blockhead," a deluded fool who voted *against* his own interests and *for* the interests of capital, refused to join a trade union and believed everything that the

2. Joe Hill, *Mister Block* (1913). [online] ProtestSongLyrics.Net. Available from *http://www.protestsonglyrics.net/*.

newspapers and politicians told him. Meanwhile he lived a hand-to-mouth existence, constantly trying to find a secure income and regularly falling for get-rich-quick schemes published in the press. A recurring storyline depicted Mr. Block believing a capitalist lie, only to be violently shown the error of his ways. In one such example, being unemployed and reading in the newspaper that there are well-paid jobs available, he tells himself "It's no use kicking about hard times. A man can get a job if he goes after it"[3] and rushes off to apply, only to be told the position has just been filled. He joins a huge crowd of men who have been given the same news. They are told by a member of the IWW that: the "Capitalist papers are printing blind ads in order to get the last penny from the unemployed." The Wobbly encourages them to read the *Industrial Worker* instead. Mr. Block does not have time to take this on board before he is hit over the head, for "Blockading the street," by the police — who decline to believe his pleas that he is a "peaceable citizen." Unfortunately, this does not teach him a lesson. Mr. Block refuses, as he says, to "condemn the whole so-called capitalist press as the IWW does. My last boss told me that the newspapers are alright and that the IWW is all wrong, it must be so."[4] Instead, he continues to be duped by advertisement after advertisement.

On another occasion it is Block's belief in the U.S.

3. Ernest Riebe, "Mr. Block. He Reads of a Good Job" (1913). Available from *http://www.iww.org/graphics/cartoons/mrblock*.
4. Ernest Riebe, *Twenty-Four Cartoons of Mr. Block* (Chicago: Charles H. Kerr Publishing Company, 1984).

justice system that is shown to be misplaced. He mocks "Some knocker," who has told him "that a poor man hasn't a chance in the courts against the rich man," and instead proclaims that "there is justice before the law under the American flag."[5] This is put to the test after he is run over by a motor car and spends two years pursuing damages. He finally wins his case, but his lawyer takes 95 percent of the money. Similarly, but more seriously, Block is taken in by the war mongering press and employers. In the cartoon "When Block meets Block" from 1914, Blocks from different countries attempt to kill each other in the name of nationalism while the (literal) vultures of capitalism look on.[6] On a separate occasion, Block becomes a wartime profiteer himself and doctors newspaper headlines in order to sell copies to different nationalities. To the French he peddles news of a French victory and thousands of German casualties; to the Germans he sells the same headline with the nationalities reversed. As always, the situation ends badly for Block: when he tries to hawk jingoistic newspapers to members of the IWW, they tell him that they deem it "an insult to take us for patriots," that the union is their only nationality and proceed to give him a kicking.[7] Mr. Block strips frequently showed xenophobia to be part of the capitalist agenda also in peacetime. In one storyline[8]

5. Ibid.

6. Ernest Riebe, "When Block Meets Block" (1914). Available from *http://www.nickthorkelson.com/mrblock.htm*.

7. Ernest Riebe, "Mr. Block Insults Members of the IWW" (1914). Available from *http://www.nickthorkelson.com/mrblock.htm*.

8. Ernest Riebe, "Mr. Block. He Meets Others" (1912). Available from

Block's "boss" encourages discord, based on ethnicity, amongst his workers (all Blocks of different nationalities) and then relaxes as his employees exchange racist abuse, incapable of uniting against him. The Wobblies were known for their stance against racism and the employers' habit of playing different nationalities of workers off against each other.

As with many socialist groups at the time, the IWW's goal was to educate the working-class so they could realize their true situation and emancipate themselves. Those who were already converted needed to be kept on side and those who were not, who were suffering from false consciousness, needed to be enlightened. To do this they employed chalk talks (illustrated lectures), speeches, readers' letters, songs, comic strips, newspaper editorials and books. The Wobblies saw songs, cartoons, and comics, in particular, as being a vital part of their activism, realizing that these could provide an effective way of transmitting a message that might otherwise easily be lost if only published in theoretical texts. While in prison on a fabricated charge of murder in 1915, Hill encapsulated the IWW strategy, reiterating the importance of humor and education in a letter, stating:

> If a person can put a few cold, common sense facts into a song and dress them up in a cloak of humor to take the dryness off of them, he will succeed in reaching a great number of workers who are too

---

http://www.iww.org/graphics/cartoons/mrblock.

> unintelligent or too indifferent to read a pamphlet or an editorial on economic science.[9]

Walker C. Smith's introduction to the Block comic book also acknowledged the power of cartoon strips in

> an age in which pictures play a leading part, an age where the moving picture show has stolen the audiences of the church and where the magazine without illustrations has fallen by the wayside, this little book of cartoons ... is sent out to catch the eye and mold the mind of any Block into whose hands it might fall.[10]

Comic strips could serve as an introduction to labor movement arguments for newcomers and act as a reminder and entertainment for activists. Not only were cartoons and comics of educational and democratic importance, they also sold well.

Mr Block's fame quickly became in international. In Australia, where there was a strong IWW movement, Hill's "Mr Block" was adapted by changing "President" to "Premier." The newspaper *Direct Action* used Riebe's character as a form of admonishment towards their readers — "Now, Mr. Block, stand up like men" — and during

9. Philip S. Foner, *The Letters of Joe Hill* (New York: Oak Publications, 1965).
10. Walker C. Smith, "Introductory," in *Twenty-four Cartoons of Mr. Block*, ed. Ernest Riebe (Chicago: Charles H. Kerr Publishing Company, 1984).

1914–15 published their own version of the Mr. Block comic strip, "The Amazing Adventures of Mr. Simple." In primarily the anglophone world, but also in other countries, such as Sweden, Mr. Block entered mainstream language as a symbol of the gullible, "blockhead" worker.

When the First World War broke out the authorities in the U.S. used the conflict as an excuse to brutally suppress the labor movement and, in particular, the IWW. The latter were accused of being traitors, of being "Imperial William's Warriors." The Wobbly anti-war organizer Frank Little was brutally murdered. IWW premises and meetings were violently raided, their publications banned, and their members arrested. The Wobblies were an anti-war organization, but they also believed that they needed to win the battle in the workplace before they could hope to influence an international conflict. Consequently, they drastically reduced their anti-war rhetoric and did not actively oppose the draft, but this had little effect on their persecution, which continued after the war with mass deportations of IWW members.

Amongst the anti-war publications that the IWW did produce was a special issue of their newspaper *Solidarity* in 1914. This included many anti-war cartoons, among them a strip by Riebe entitled "Poor Mother." Poor Mother did not share Mr. Block's distinctive head form but was otherwise very similar. A working-class woman, she is so "enthusiastic about militarism and capitalism" that she happily sends her son off to war.[11]

11. Ernest Riebe, "Poor Mother," *Solidarity*, October 31, 1914.

If he survives, she is overjoyed and doesn't care that other women's sons have been killed; if he dies, however, writes Riebe, "she's squealing for sympathy and — strange — she gets it."

After the war Mr. Block reappeared for a time in the revived *Industrial Worker* and *Solidarity* and twice in book form, the *Crimes of the Bolsheviki* and *Mr. Block and the Profiteers*, both published in 1919. The former was written in support of the Russian Revolution and featured Block as a foolish newspaper reader believing such reports as "Bolsheviki declare women in Russia state property ... Rape legalized."[12] During the 1920s the IWW were almost destroyed, and Block ceased to appear. He has lived on, however, in Hill's song, in reprinted comic strips and as a descriptive term for a foolish worker. In recent years he has appeared in the book *Wobblies: A Graphic History*,[13] freshly drawn by Nick Thorkelson, and now he has become the fortunate star of erotic adventures, hardly something Riebe could have imagined when he first drew Mr. Block over a century ago. Block remains contemporary; in an era of "false news" he is as depressingly recognizable a figure today as he was in 1912. The fictional Mr. Block will therefore hopefully continue educating and entertaining for a further hundred years.

— Anna Hoyles, PhD, University of Lincoln (UK)

12. Ernest Riebe, *Crimes of the Bolsheviki: Dedicated to the Interests of the International Proletariat* (Chicago: All-American Publishing Co. Not Inc., 1919).
13. Paul Buhle and Nicole Schulman, *Wobblies! A Graphic History of the Industrial Workers of the World* (London: Verso, 2005).

STRIKE

Characters

CLIFFORD: a worker.

VICTORIA: a worker.

BENEDICT: a worker.

CARLA: a worker.

EMMA: a worker.

GEORGE: a worker—
later promoted to foreman.

DON: a worker—
he wears a fine moustache.

AGGIE: an outside agitator.

REARMAN: the foreman—
later fired.

EVELYN SACKS: the boss (of the local XYZ, Inc. branch).

ALLEN SACKS: the boss's boss and husband (corporate managing director of XYZ, Inc.).

JULIA SACKS: the boss's and the boss's boss's daughter.

RONALD DUMP: the boss's boss's boss (CEO of XYZ, Inc.).

SMELANIA DUMP: the boss's boss's boss and wife (CEO of XYZ Group, which owns XYZ, Inc.).

THEODORE DUMP: the boss's boss's boss's and the boss's boss's boss's boss's son.

FLORIAN MOFFAT: majority shareholder of XYZ Group and chairman of its board.

A WAITRESS.

A BAND.

MISTER BLOCK: a worker.

... but don't tell that to him. He's new on the job. He also has a big wooden block for a head.

Overture

As the band plays the first few instrumental bars of "Mr. Block" by Joe Hill, programs are distributed to the audience. They read, "MR. BLOCK, starring in Praise Boss!" And under this: "A managerial sex tragicomedy in three acts (a comedy for Mr. Block, a tragedy for the working class)." There is no mention of Acts IV and V. Beneath an illustration of the blockheaded hero, a caption reads, "He sleeps his way to the top." The flip side of the program includes the words to a couple of songs in praise of Mr. Block, so you can sing along when the band plays them during intermission. A stack of extra programs is left on the edge of the stage. When the band stops playing, a janitor walks across the stage in front of the closed curtain, mopping the floor and pulling a bucket on wheels while humming "Mr. Block." The janitor is Aggie.

AGGIE: (*singing to herself*)

Please give me your attention, I'll introduce to you
A man that is a credit to "Our Red, White, and Blue";
His head is made of lumber, and solid as a rock;
He is a common worker, and his name is—

(*She notices the stack of programs.*) Say, what's this? (*Picking one up and reading*) Mr. Block! Well I'd be damned, if I weren't already. That sapsucker's still around! And after all these years he still thinks he can make it to the top! He's tried just about everything the bosses tell him to do, and still he can't hold a job. Every time he falls back down, broke as a beggar, broke as a CEO pretends to be when the beggars come around! Broke as a broker ought to be—hey, what's that sound? (*She looks offstage, stage left.*) Well, there he is right now! Working away! If only the guy who wrote his song were here today, he'd help Block get wise. (*She stops for a moment to think.*) But then, maybe the old songwriter never really died. (*She reaches into her bucket and pulls out a broad-brimmed hat and a ragged blazer. When she puts them on, she's the spitting image of Joe Hill—that is, if the bosses noticed how much she looks like him, they'd spit at her. The blazer also has a big nametag reading "HILL."*) So let's get to it. Now I wonder, is there anything—other than solidarity—that this blockhead still hasn't tried?

She mops the other flyers off the stage and leaves as the curtains open.

Act I.

Monday. At the local branch of XYZ, Inc.

scene 1

As the curtain opens, we see a windowless room furnished with two large plastic tables, cheap folding chairs, two vending machines, and a counter that will later serve as the company canteen. On the back wall, under a clock, is a column of portraits labeled in large letters: at the bottom is branch boss Evelyn Sacks; above her, corporate managing director Allen Sacks; above him is CEO of XYZ, Inc. Ronald Dump; above him, CEO of XYZ Group Smelania Dump; at the top is majority owner and board chair Florian Moffat. There are two doors, one stage left, opening to the work room, and one stage right, opening to the boss's office. Beyond the work room, where the lights are currently off, there is a door leading outside. Clifford, Victoria, Benedict, Carla, Emma, and George come from the dark work room into the break room and sit down. Clifford, wearing a hooded sweatshirt and jeans with holes, leans back and kicks his legs up on another chair. Benedict, who might be wearing a heavy cross around his neck, or perhaps a T-shirt silkscreened with a picture of Jesus, picks up a magazine of conservative bent, something like The Weekly Substandard or The Daily Drab or National Conservative. Victoria, sitting near Clifford, is dressed darkly, maybe entirely in black. Her hair is dyed black. Maybe even her makeup is black.

VICTORIA: (*with a frown that she'll keep up through most of the play*) I hate Mondays.

CLIFFORD: (*with a nonchalance that is as dear to him as worry is to Victoria*) Oh, I worship 'em.

BENEDICT: (*with a haughty scowl*) How's that? You're late every Monday.

CLIFFORD: Yeah, I'm busy worshiping Saint Monday. (*He yawns.*) Still am.

Don enters. His sharp and flashy clothing, well-sculpted hair, and carefully curled moustache stand out against the dull surroundings of XYZ, Inc. He is as confident in his own irresistibility as he is unable to resist flirting with those around him.

DON: (*to the men*) You're looking lovely today! (*to the women*) You're not too shabby either. It is nice to see you all! I do apologize. I would have helped you all at work, but other responsibilities called.

BENEDICT: Responsible you call it?

DON: It would've been selfish to abandon the poor young lady so early in the morning. Priorities are priorities.

CARLA: (*Though she rolls her eyes, she never stops cheerfully smiling. Then she notices something.*) Hey, where's the new guy? Did he get lost on the way to the break room?

Block enters. He does not take a seat, which forces those around him into the awkward position of standing back up to speak to him.

BLOCK: Is it break time already? I was just getting started.

CARLA: What was your name?

BLOCK: Block.

GEORGE: (*George speaks softly, but with the air of someone who knows what he's doing and wants to help others so they know what they're doing too. His overalls show signs of wear.*) We're happy to have you here, Mr. Block. We could really use another set of hands around here. Another head too. My name's George. This is Carla. And over here—

BLOCK: (*ignoring the introductions, not noticing the hands offered to be shaken*) I am glad to be here! My father always said having a job is a blessing ...

BENEDICT: (*putting down his magazine*) God put us on this earth to work.

CLIFFORD: Then why'd He make us in His image? Don't see God doing much work.

BLOCK: ... and I must be really blessed, because I've had hundreds of jobs.

CLIFFORD: (*horrified*) One is too much for me!

GEORGE: Where were you working before you came here?

BLOCK: Customer service for a dating app. Nice work. A pleasure bringing people together, you know. The lonely with the lonely, the bored with the bored, the owner with his money. Seeing 'em together, I knew they'd never part. Made me chief operating officer of computer 137.

CARLA: (*impressed by the sound of Block's title*) Wow! Then why'd you leave?

BLOCK: Too easy. A hard-working man needs to sweat a little.

BENEDICT: I know it. (*Raises his arm and takes in his body odor. Carla, next to him, recoils.*)

BLOCK: Also, they fired me.

BENEDICT: I knew it.

BLOCK: I was the best agent on the job, no doubt. Just the trouble. People'd message me asking for help, and all of a sudden they're in love with the customer service agent who answers all their Q's with A's so fine they left the app and went straight for me.

CARLA: Really?

BLOCK: One day the boss comes up and says, "Block, you're my best worker. Hell, you could even have my job if I didn't have it myself. But this won't do."

GEORGE: He let a good employee go, just like that?

BLOCK: We came to an understanding. Said I should take my talents somewhere that's ready for me, where I can really advance.

CLIFFORD: (*incredulous*) So you came here?

BLOCK: Not directly. First I took a job over at the Fritz. Vice-executive porteur was my official title, but I never let my head get too square about it. Just a matter of logistics, making sure things get where they need to go. Serving the customer, whoever it was. I'd provide the same service to Joe-Motel-6 as I'd give to Jess Besos or the executive board of Oldman Sacks.

BENEDICT: That's humility for you.

BLOCK: But Besos always did ask for me, facts are facts. I'm just sayin'. Besos, Musk, Odor, you name 'em, I served 'em. They'd come to the concierge and say, "Get me Block. I can't have just anyone's paws on my équipage." (*The workers nod, impressed.*) Well, my boss was about to promote me to principle executive porteur, thank you very much, hard work pays, you know. But one day this gentleman shows up, a sharp-looking suit, hair all coiffed, clearly a man of means—but of ends, too, as it turned out.

VICTORIA: (*as usual, frowning*) Uh, oh. How'd it end?

BLOCK: Well now I'd already been requested by Ronald Dump himself, he was waiting for me on the other side of the lobby. I could see him there. I could see a hundred Dumps reflected in all the mirrors and shiny railings and fresh-waxed floor, all waiting and tapping their feet, getting anxious. But my boss he comes and says, "Block, I need you to help this other fellow over here. You're the only one we can trust with the job." So I say hell, Ronald can wait. I take the other guy's bags to his room, and he gives me a hundred bucks to carry just one more bag for him. To an address all the way across town.

GEORGE: Your boss let you go across town?

BLOCK: Let me? Why, he begged me! But when I show up at the place, the police are there. They open the bag, and it's filled with money, crisp, like straight from the laundry. Trafficking, they said. "Traffic?" I say. "Damn , next time I'll just take the subway."

VICTORIA: Your boss got you mixed up in trafficking? I bet you told him where to shove it.

BLOCK: We came to a mutual understanding.

CARLA: Wow.

BLOCK: I took all the blame and jail time. He gave me the number of a friend who runs a roofing business so I could call for a job when I got out.

BENEDICT: Reasonable.

BLOCK: I'd hardly seen the light of day, and I was already getting tan on the roofs. The sun would shine down from above and up from below, reflecting off the shingles. I told my boss, "You should open a tanning salon up here." He said, "Block, I like the way you think." I said, "So do I." He gave me tougher and tougher jobs, and lowered my salary too—said he was deducting the value of the grade-A tan he gave me. Every day he'd ask me, "Are you ready to take things to the next level?" and I'd tell him, "By Boss, I'm going all the way to the top!"

BENEDICT: That's the spirit.

BLOCK: One day I went right through the roof.

CLIFFORD: That's one way to get to the top.

BLOCK: No, I fell down through the roof. (*Pause.*) We came to an understanding.

CLIFFORD: You and your boss?

BLOCK: No, me and the lady I fell on. I nearly broke her back. And her whole boudoir. But the boudoir came later. She said, "Your boss won't want you back after this. If you stay and work off what you owe me from the fall, I won't sue."

CLIFFORD: What did she have you do?

BLOCK: I don't need to bore you with details. A man's work is never easy, but I thank Boss for all the jobs I've had the privilege to have.

BENEDICT: Damn right. That's what I always tell them. We should stop complaining and thank God for everything He gives.

BLOCK: Thank who?

BENEDICT: Thank God, just like you said, fella.

BLOCK: God, God ... (*thinks it over*) ... no, can't say the name rings a bell. But if he gives you jobs, sounds all right by me. Speaking of bells ... (*looks at the clock on the wall*) ... we'd better get back to work!

Block jumps up and begins to walk toward the door to the work room. The others remain seated. Before reaching the door, Block turns to the audience and begins a monologue.

BLOCK: The first day on the job, the best day on the job! Everything lies before you! With an emphasis on the lies. Like the sun rising on the horizon. With an emphasis on the hor–." Ah, work! What a piece of work you are! So handsome to behold! So fine to have had done! So fetching to pretend to do. And yet so hard to get to be the one to make another do it! Just think of how it'll sound, some day—"Mister Block, by the sap of his log, he worked his way to the top!" Suffering sack-o-cash, if only they'd let me work long enough to finish the story. That's the thing! Ah, work, that strange, obscure nectar! When you don't have it, your tongue grows dry with thirst. And when you smell it, you waste no time, you pounce! You drink like it like a lion lost out in the desert, coming to a hidden watering hole. So sweet to behold, but it burns in the throat. You drink so much, it's like you're breathing fire! And then then, in an instant, it's gone. Snuffed out. Drenched and doused, you flop once more beneath the thirsty sun. You say: I'm done! I've had my share. Let others take that poison drink, for all I care. But damn, that sun is hot, I'm parched again. One last job, you say. Let's do it right this time, and then ... They say hard work will take you far. And after all, every job is easy if your head is hard. I've had a hundred of 'em (jobs, I mean, not heads). Was moving my way up a hundred times! Could've been a hundred CEOs! What's that? "Mister Block," you say? But listen now, at the end of this amazing race, how sweet the sound! "Chief Block!" "Executive Block!" "Officer

Block!" If only another thing or two had gone my way. By Boss, I've got to try. This time's the time. This time I'll rise. This time I'm going up! By hook or else by crook! With an emphasis on the crook.

The band plays for a few moments as Block heads toward the work room door. But before he or the other workers leave the break room, Scene 2 begins. (The band will play a few seconds to mark the end of every scene.)

scene 2

Aggie bursts into the break room from the front of the stage (avoiding the doors to the work room and the boss's office). She's still wearing Joe Hill's hat and blazer, but now, without a nametag, she could be taken for a 1910s Bible pusher. She speaks with the speed of someone who knows that the authorities might come at any moment to shut her up.

AGGIE: Praise the Worker, I have found you!

The workers turn toward her.

GEORGE: (*Politely*) Good morning. Who is it you were looking for?

AGGIE: I'm looking for people who are looking, and I see them right before me! Are you feeling down? Forlorn? Hungry for something more in life? When you get up in the morning, have you got nothing but up, and barely even that? You wonder, bell, is that all there is, just a bell to start off the day, and nothing more? You want meaning, but all you find is meanness. You want to sit in the garden of eatin', but you're herded in and out of the room of breaking, in and out until you're nearly broke!

GEORGE: I'm sorry, are you sure you're in the right place?

AGGIE: I'm as sure as the workday is long! (*She takes out a roll of agitational posters and passes them around.*) I can see it on your faces, in their reflection on the vending machine glass! I can see it on the windowless walls that bear no reflection! I can see it in the room next door, in the total dark! (*She gestures to the work room, where the lights are now off.*) I could see it in your foreman's sneer when I came knocking, saying, "Sir, I'm a minister of morale, an infuser of industrial inspiration! I'm a tinker of workplace worry! I'll hammer it into happiness! I have the means to turn complaining to creation, burnout into born-again! It's in the Book!" I say. (*She winks.*) He says, "Then right this way."

BENEDICT: Tell us a little something from the Good Book. Maybe it'll teach these guys to quit complaining.

AGGIE: Ah, but mine isn't a Good Book. It's a bad book. It's no book of satisfaction. It's a book of discontent. It doesn't render Caesar what he's owed, it takes it back. It's not a Great Book. It's a little book. It isn't black and white. It's red. It doesn't preach. It sings. (*She takes from her pocket a little red songbook.*)

EMMA: (*Emma, though generally quiet, reserved, and serious, is now amused.*) Let's hear it sing.

AGGIE: (*taking a few more copies of the book from her shoulder bag and passing them around*) Did you hear about the boss who went to heaven? (They shake their heads.) Me neither.

Aggie leads them in the so-called "Wobbly Doxology" (to the tune of the hymn "Praise God, from Whom All Blessings Flow"):

Praise Boss when morning work bells chime,
Praise Him for bits of overtime,
Praise Him when He forgets to pay,
Praise Him, and then toss him away!

Aw hell.

The last line is pronounced with the intonation of "Amen." Most of them laugh. Benedict is uncomfortable.

BLOCK: (*without irony*) Praise boss!

AGGIE: Did you hear about the worker who went to heaven? (*Again they shake their heads.*) Me neither.

Foreman Rearman arrives.

REARMAN: All right, time to work! (*turning to Aggie*) Thanks for your inspiration. Come again. Now let's work with twice the verve, eh?

Benedict tries to speak, to tell him what Aggie has really been saying to them, but Rearman cuts him off and waves him into the work room. The others slowly follow, except for Block, who rushes ahead and enters the work room first. Rearman pushes Aggie out the way she came.

scene 3

The lights go on in the work room. On the side of the room opposite the break room door, there are two small windows and another door that leads outside. The band plays while all the workers other than Block are busily engaged in activities of unclear and irrelevant purpose (one might be at a computer, another at a large machine, another muttering into a phone, another packing unidentifiable objects into box and tossing it out the window, etc.). Rearman walks around, looking over their shoulders. Block excitedly wanders about looking for something to do. He tries to join his co-workers in the jobs they are already doing, but he gets in their way, and they keep waving him away. Finally, satisfied that he's tried his best, Block sits down in the corner. The music stops.

REARMAN: (*seeing Block idling in the corner*) Block! Get back to work.

BLOCK: (*jumping to attention and saluting*) By Boss! There's nothing I'd rather do! Why, sir, my whole life's work is work! Only, I don't know exactly what we're doing here.

REARMAN: You're working for our boss, Ms. Evelyn Sacks, and you do what she tells you to.

BLOCK: Just what I most like doing! So what does she tell me to do?

REARMAN: She tells you to do what I tell you to do.

BLOCK: Perfect! The chain of command—the happiest chain for any man.

REARMAN: And I tell you to get to work!

BLOCK: Just what I was telling myself! What work should I do?

REARMAN: For God's sake, Block, the boss doesn't pay me to stand here all day talking to you. Find some work and do it.

BLOCK: (*still cheerful*) Just what I was talking to you about, in fact!

At this moment the lunch bell rings. While all the workers except Block rush out the door to the break room, Block keeps speaking to Rearman.

BLOCK: Just one word from you, Mr. Foreman Rearman, and I'll work for days on end! Work itself is my daily bread. And it never gets stale. At least until they make me boss.

Rearman hesitates, briefly pretending to be as indifferent to lunch as he is annoyed by Block. But then he too rushes off after the others. He turns off the work room light as he leaves. Block waits behind in the dark for a bit but finally follows the others to lunch.

---

scene 4

Rearman, having cut to the front of the line at the counter, gets his lunch and sits down by himself. The others get their lunches and sit down together at a second table. Block and George are the last still standing. George, seeing that the chair next to Emma is free, walks toward it, but he hesitates. Though he is confident in everything related to work, all his self-confidence disappears when he looks at Emma. Block, last in line, takes his lunch to Rearman's table, but Rearman waves him away. Just as George is finally about to sit down next to Emma, Block takes his place. George sits next to Block. For a few moments, they all eat quietly. Then George breaks the silence.

GEORGE: (*Leaning forward, he speaks past Block to Emma.*) You doing anything this evening?

Emma leans to speak past Block, but Block answers instead.

BLOCK: Sorry associate, but I need to keep my free time free, so I can spend it getting ready for work.

EMMA: (*ignoring Block*) I don't know.

GEORGE: (*nervous*) I was just thinking, I mean, just, if you wanted to hang out for a bit, I mean ... It's my birthday today ...

CARLA: (*overhearing them*) It's your birthday, George? We have to celebrate! Let's go out somewhere. We'll ask the boss to let us off early.

GEORGE: (*both disappointed and relieved*) Yeah, sure, we should all go out.

DON: But Carla, why don't we leave the lovebirds to themselves? If you need company tonight, I—

BENEDICT: God spare us all your talk of "love."

DON: Love is the great transformer. It makes the downcast happy. It makes the empty full. It makes the dirty clean.

BENEDICT: I hope you use soap too.

DON: (*ignoring Benedict's remark*) It makes blind men see, makes villains friends, turns beggars into rich men and makes rich men beg for more.

BENEDICT: Makes executives promote their mistresses.

EMMA: Don't start with that again.

DON: Our boss put her heart into her work. There's nothing wrong with that.

EMMA: Every time a woman is successful, people say she's slept her way up.

Benedict is on the point of saying something impolite about the boss when Aggie enters, disguised as a delivery worker, carrying a cardboard box big enough to hold a pie.

AGGIE: Delivery!

REARMAN: Did anyone order anything?

They all shake their heads.

AGGIE: I have an order right here: one pie in the sky, ordered by Ms. Evelyn Sacks for her workers. (*I understand she's your boss. Very thoughtful of her.*)

BLOCK: Oh, my, Mrs. Sacks, she shouldn't have!

REARMAN: But I don't know if ...

BLOCK: Let's see it!

AGGIE: Come and take it.

GEORGE: (*hesitant*) Is there enough to go around?

AGGIE: You'll all get your share!

They approach, and Aggie places the cardboard box on the table. Block jumps in front of the others and opens the box. It's empty.

BLOCK: What's this?

AGGIE: It's just what boss is giving you! You ask for a raise, a vacation, you name it—she orders you a pie in the sky.

VICTORIA: Can we place a different order?

AGGIE: Can you ever! The possibilities are endless. A belly full of delicacies. A platter of good pay. A workplace floor so fine you could eat off it. A breakfast—no, a brunch—of brotherhood. Sisterhood for supper. A lunch of longings finally fulfilled. No cottony clouds, but whipped-up cream. No hollow crust, but a life that's full!

REARMAN: (*pushing Aggie out of the room*) Get out of here. We don't need your kind of deliverance.

BLOCK: So when do we get our pie in the sky?

AGGIE: (*stopping on the way out*) When you die.

Aggie leaves. The boss, Evelyn Sacks, enters. She wears a power suit. Maybe off-white or beige.

EVELYN: Who was that?

REARMAN: Someone must have called in a crank order. I've sent her away.

EVELYN: Good. I don't want her distracting us again.

She walks back to her office. Block tries to catch her attention as she leaves.

BLOCK: Ms. Boss! I am so glad to see you! May I thank you for your generosity and ask you to consider giving your most devoted employee (*at this point she has already entered the office and closes the door in Block's face*) a promotion?

The bell rings, and the workers head into the work room. Block is slow to respond, but then he rushes ahead of the others and is the first to enter the work room.

scene 5

The band plays as the workers resume their earlier tasks. This time, Block has a task too. Maybe he has a giant tablet and spends his time swiping the screen left, right, up, down, turning it over, shaking it, palming it, licking it ... Don is next to Carla, and he repeatedly leans over and whispers to her, provoking amusement. Benedict is on Carla's other side, and she repeatedly leans over and whispers to him, provoking discomfort. Clifford is next to Victoria, and he repeatedly leans over and whispers to her, to which she replies by shaking her head. When he's not busy whispering to Victoria, Clifford yawns. George has managed to place himself next to Emma, and he repeatedly looks at her when she's not looking. He turns away when she looks his way. Only Block resolutely concentrates on his work. Rearman walks around the room, looking over the shoulder of one after another of the workers. Each time Rearman is near, the worker in question abruptly pretends to be concentrating on work—except for Block, who instead turns to smile at Rearman, who angrily tells him to get back to work. This goes on for a while, until suddenly Rearman freezes, gazing out one of the windows. The music stops, but for some time the other workers take no notice of Rearman. Finally, Block goes to see what's going on.

BLOCK: Foreman Rearman! Is everything OK?

Rearman ignores him and continues gazing out the window. His head slowly turns, following something that is passing by outside. Then, without looking at Block, he moves to the other window and continues gazing.

BLOCK: (*more loudly*) Foreman Rearman, most excellent sir, embodiment of Bossiness! What is it?

Rearman still ignores Block and continues turning his head, watching something outside.

BLOCK: (*still more loudly*) Foreman Rearman, tell us what's befallen us? I'm ready to take on anything!

As suddenly as he entered his daze, Rearman snaps out of it.

REARMAN: (*even more loudly than Block*) Block, get back to work!

Block returns sheepishly to his work space and resumes his earlier task. Don, next to him, notices his embarrassment.

DON: Don't sweat it, my friend.

BLOCK: I don't know what's gotten into him.

DON: It's not what's gotten into him. It's what he'd like to get into her.

BLOCK: Of course. Into who?

DON: That was the boss's daughter who just walked by.

scene 6

Aggie enters, disguised as a repair worker, carrying a box of tools and whistling to herself. Foreman Rearman turns to her.

AGGIE: Heard the call. System's broke.

REARMAN: (*not seeing through the disguise*) Who called?

AGGIE: Oh, it could've been anyone. It's obvious. Look around.

REARMAN: (*after looking around*) I don't think our systems need fixing.

AGGIE: Just what I tried to tell 'em! The system can't be fixed. It was broken from the start. Here, let me show you.

She begins to remove agitational materials from her tool box: pamphlets, songbooks, buttons, all bright red and black. Rearman doesn't notice.

REARMAN: (*to the workers*) Keep working! I'll handle this.

He begins walking around the room, fiddling with the computers, checking a modem on the floor, opening an electrical box by the door, looking into an outlet on the wall.

AGGIE: (*to the workers*) Sorry folks, but this is serious. You're gonna have to take a break. Your work keeps the broken system going. The only way to fix it is to stop, so the system stops, so you can open it up and poke around and see how dusty and corroded and mixed up and crissed and crossed it is on the inside. Might have to pull out all its wiring and throw it in the trash and put a whole new set in place!

The workers stop working and slowly gather around Aggie. Rearman, still trying to find the problem, doesn't notice.

CARLA: (*reading one of the pamphlets*) Hey, so you're talking about ...

AGGIE: That's right, fellow workers, I'm talking about the wage system! You know the one. You live it every day. The system part, that is. The wages come less often.

Evelyn Sacks enters.

EVELYN: What's going on here?

REARMAN: (*calling out from the corner*) System's down!

EVELYN: (*turning to Aggie*) Who are you?

AGGIE: I only bring the tools. But I can't fix the system myself. And neither can you, I'm afraid, Ms. Boss. Only the workers can, when they pick up the tools themselves.

EVELYN: (*Suspicious*) What tools?

AGGIE: Power tools!

EVELYN: (*to the workers*) All right now, back to work!

AGGIE: That's right! Don't stand around doing nothing. People will start thinking you're the boss!

EVELYN: (*turning to Aggie*) Out! Hey! (*recognizing her as the agitator from before*) You're the ... (*Turning to Rearman*) Rearman!

REARMAN: Let me just check one more thing.

EVELYN: Rearman! Did you let her back in? I gave you one simple order: get everyone to work without distraction.

Rearman hangs his head. Aggie bows with a smile and makes her way toward the door. Before leaving she turns back.

AGGIE: What's the difference between a boss and a battery?

REARMAN and **BLOCK:** (*at the same time*) I never thought about ...

AGGIE: Batteries have plus sides.

EVELYN: (*turning her fury to Rearman*) Take her out! I don't want to see her here again. (*She pauses.*) Or you either. Go!

Aggie slips out. Rearman follows slowly.

scene 7

Block knocks on the door of the boss's office, which is located on the opposite side of the break room. Without waiting for a reply, he enters. Evelyn is seated behind a large desk.

BLOCK: Praise Boss, boss, I know you'll stand with me!

EVELYN: (*not looking up*) I'm not standing.

BLOCK: Indeed, you're humble, you're closer to the lowly, you'll sit with me, then (*looks around in vain for a chair*)—or you'll raise me up! That's what I've come to ask of you in my hour of need.

EVELYN: Three thirty?

BLOCK: Three thirty an hour, three forty-five, it doesn't matter. I'm not in it for the money. It's the—

EVELYN: Get out.

BLOCK: Yes! O Boss, get me out! Get me out of this pit of lazy labor, and make a foreman out of me!

Evelyn finally looks up at him.

BLOCK: (*Block's voice gradually grows quieter as he speaks.*) I've worked hard, all the hot, long day, all of it so far, I mean, and I mean to work the rest of it too and then some, but I seek a newer, higher work. I want to rise above myself and others. You must understand. You've risen too. They say you came ... came up through the ranks; they say you were on the bottom and ended up on top. (*At this point Block can barely be heard over the band, which begins to play the "Wobbly Doxology."*) You were prone, yet now you sit. You lay so that you could stand. From the flimsy matter that was given to you, you erected a whole career. I ask much less. I see a need, that's all, and I have a need. I see a hole, and I need to fill it. Let me fill your vacancy. (*Now the lights dim in the boss's office. Block drones quietly on.*) What I request is little, but I offer much. I will ...

The band stops playing as the lights go on now in the break room, where the other workers are gathered.

CARLA: (*to George*) She couldn't say no to you. You're her best employee!

VICTORIA: Has she ever given us anything we asked for?

EMMA: We worked late every day last week.

CARLA: And George only has a birthday once a year.

GEORGE: All right. I'll ask her.

CARLA: (*looking at George, who still hasn't moved*) Well?

As George goes timidly to the boss's office, the lights go off in the break room and come on in the office. Block is still speaking.

BLOCK: … I'll follow every rule there is to follow. I'll break every rule that must be broken. I'd go to the ends of the earth to climb just one rung on your ladder. I'll crack every whip for you, hammer every nail, turn every screw, screw every …

EVELYN: (*seeing George*) I'm so glad you came.

BLOCK and **GEORGE:** (*simultaneously*) You are?

EVELYN: Very much so.

GEORGE: The other folks and I were just thinking …

EVELYN: (*interrupting him*) You are aware that Foreman Rearman has moved on.

GEORGE: Yes, but I think we've picked up the slack quite well. We've already …

EVELYN: This means I need a new foreman.

BLOCK: Very much so. In fact, we were just discussing that matter …

EVELYN: You're my most dependable employee.

BLOCK and **GEORGE:** (*simultaneously*) Thank you.

EVELYN: I'm offering you a promotion.

BLOCK: Thank … (*He does not finish, because in the meantime Evelyn has stood up and shaken George's hand.*)

Block stands gaping. So does George.

EVELYN: Wonderful. Now let's get back to business. There's still an hour and a half before five. Let's add another after that to make up for lost time.

GEORGE: But …

EVELYN: What?

GEORGE: Nothing. I mean, thank you.

George walks slowly out. Block remains behind, still agape, until Evelyn clears her throat and George gently pulls him out.

---

scene 8

George and Block enter the break room. The others look up at George hopefully.

DON: What's the word?

GEORGE: (*without enthusiasm*) I got a promotion.

CARLA: Wahoo! Double celebration!

CLIFFORD: Drinks on you, Mr. Just-Got-a-Raise!

EMMA: What's wrong, George?

GEORGE: I didn't get us off early. Sacks told us to stay an hour late instead.

The workers shuffle slowly toward the work room. Emma and George pause for a moment.

EMMA: It's still great news.

GEORGE: I guess so.

EMMA: You'll be a good foreman.

GEORGE: I still wanted to hang out with you guys. I mean, especially with ... (*He doesn't finish.*)

EMMA: What?

GEORGE: I was just thinking. If you still have time when we get off work ...

Evelyn enters.

EVELYN: George, they just called in from headquarters. They need a hundred design prototypes by tomorrow. Sorry about this. Just another two or three hours should be enough to finish it all.

GEORGE: All right, I'll tell them.

George and Emma leave for the work room, Evelyn to her office.

scene 9

In the work room, no one is concentrating on work.

BLOCK: Sham it to sell, I expected a little more respect.

VICTORIA: I don't expect anything from that whore.

EMMA: She's not a whore.

DON: We all sell ourselves. It's just a matter of choosing clients and conditions.

VICTORIA: Have you seen Mr. Sacks? (*She points to his portrait on the wall.*) No one would sleep with him unless they were aiming for a promotion. She started out working right here where we are. Then she hooks up with the corporate managing director and suddenly she's running this place!

EMMA: But she didn't sleep with CEO Dump. He's even higher up the corporate ladder.

All the workers consult the column of portraits now and continue to do so throughout the rest of this discussion.

VICTORIA: We don't know she didn't try.

DON: Or with Mrs. Dump. She's even higher up than her husband.

VICTORIA: I bet she went straight to the top and tried to get in with the chairman of the board.

BENEDICT: Florian Moffat? He'd never let her near him! They say he's a good Christian man. If he knew what was going on in this company, he'd come down and clean it all right up.

GEORGE: Come on, folks, let's try to be done here before midnight.

They finally start working. Block is next to Don.

BLOCK: (*to Don*) Is it true?

DON: If it involves love, it must be true.

BLOCK: So the surest way to rise up in this company is to ... satisfy your boss?

DON: Sure.

BLOCK: (*To the audience*) By Boss, the way is clear! If she could do it, then what have I got to fear? By folly, the bed's the place—in which I'll win the old rat race!

DON: Just be careful it's you, and not your boss, who ends up on top.

The curtain closes as the band strikes up "Mr. Block."

Act II.

Tuesday. At the boss's house.

scene 1

As the curtain opens, we see Block and Don in front of a house with two dark windows, each almost as large as a whole room. The front door is visible, stage left.

BLOCK: Help me, Mr. Don, to win my way into the boss's ... (*He searches for the right word.*)

DON: (*waving for Block to be silent*) I understand. Look closely. (*pointing to his heart*) The key to women's affection is here.

Block reaches into Don's breast pocket.

BLOCK: It's empty!

DON: Then look here. (*points to Block's heart*)

Block feels around his own breast pocket. He finds nothing.

DON: Not there. Look underneath. If you want to touch a woman's, you've got to learn to touch your own.

Block fondles his breast through his shirt.

BLOCK: You mean to say that men also have ... ?

DON: Hearts? Some men do.

Block reflects on this.

DON: Listen, Block, if you want to win a woman, you have to understand her.

BLOCK: Stand under her? I'd lie beneath her feet.

DON: Let's put it this way: What is woman?

BLOCK: I never thought to ask her.

DON: Woman is a lonely lighthouse. (*Block nods.*) By day she watches quietly. At night she shines. (*Block nods more enthusiastically.*) Woman is an ocean wind. (*Block nods.*) She blows cold for weeks on end. But still she blows. (*Block scratches his chin.*) Woman is a delicate flower. (*Block nods.*) She'll wilt if you pluck her and leave her bottom dry. (*Block scratches his head.*) Woman is a wild mare. (*Block nods enthusiastically.*) When she says neigh, she means neigh. (*Block scratches his chin again.*) Woman is the greatest thing that ever happened to man.

BLOCK: Then what is man?

DON: Man is the same. But one thing at a time. Let's focus. Think, now. What do women want?

BLOCK: I don't know.

DON: They want the same things as men.

BLOCK: Women?

DON: Sometimes. But this is the thing: every woman is one of a kind. You have to find out what she wants. Maybe she wants good company.

BLOCK: She already has a good company.

DON: She might want love.

BLOCK: I love her company.

DON: Good, then keep her company.

BLOCK: I'd love to, if only I could acquire it.

DON: Tell me, Block. What is it you like about her?

BLOCK: Her power.

DON: Tell her you admire her skill and accomplishments. Ask her about her current undertakings.

BLOCK: I'd like to be overtaking her.

DON: Hm. What else has made you fall for her?

BLOCK: I also admire her position.

DON: Missionary?

BLOCK: Exactly! I see her as a missionary, spreading the gospel of Boss! She tells us to lead a life of poverty and obey all Her commands.

DON: Listen, Block, she'll be getting here soon. I want to help you, but I can only do so much.

BLOCK: Just tell me how you do it yourself. What's the secret to success with women?

DON: Women are a paradox. I invite them to a restaurant, and they invite me home. I praise their tasty cooking, and they stop eating. I applaud their witty tongues, and they press their fingers to my mouth. I speak well of their done-up hair, and they let it down. I admire their long, soft dresses, and they drop them to the floor.

As Don's monologue grows long, Block begins to look anxiously at his watch and offstage, to see if Evelyn is coming.

DON: (*continuing unabated*) Women are a paradox, true, yet they're no mystery. There's only one path to their hearts, and it's plain for all to see. I see it, and I follow it, and I shout aloud for all to follow me. The path to women is the path to ourselves! Women treat me well because I treat them well. They labor for my love because I love their labors. They reveal their innermost thoughts to me because I hide nothing from them. They bare themselves to me because I bare my soul to them. By being myself, I can be whatever they need of me.

Block is clearly paying no attention as he looks around for signs of Evelyn's arrival.

DON: Or maybe it's my moustache.

BLOCK: (*suddenly attentive again*) Then give me your moustache, for Boss's sake! She'll be here any minute now!

Don peels off his moustache and gives it to Block.

BLOCK: Let me go and put this on. If she comes while I'm gone, keep her outside until I get back.

DON: Sure. But hurry.

BLOCK: I'll just be a minute. (*Then he looks down at his crotch and motions to indicate a need to relieve himself.*) Or two.

Block disappears behind the house, stage right. As soon as he's gone, Evelyn appears, stage left.

DON: Good afternoon!

EVELYN: (*surprised*) Ah! Hello. You're the one they call ... ?

DON: Don.

EVELYN: Yes, of course. You've shaved. I've heard a lot about you from the women at the office.

DON: They are so kind. I'm sorry you and I never had the occasion to make proper acquaintance, Ms. Sacks.

EVELYN: Evelyn. If what they say about you is true, then I'm sure the loss is mine. Please come in.

DON: Thank you very much, Ms. ... Evelyn. But give me a moment to tell you why I've come.

EVELYN: It will be more comfortable to tell me indoors. Let me offer you something to drink.

DON: That's very generous. In fact, it was a certain thirst that I came to speak to you about.

EVELYN: I've heard about your thirst.

DON: But today it's not my own thirst of which I speak.

EVELYN: So you came to hear of mine?

DON: I ... of course. The least a man can do is listen.

EVELYN: I've been miserable ever since I was made boss.

DON: We have so much in common.

EVELYN: But this is no place for talking. Come inside.

DON: I suppose it wouldn't hurt to have a look inside ...

Don takes a step toward the door but stops again, looking off in the direction where Block disappeared.

EVELYN: What is it?

DON: I've forgotten something.

EVELYN: A boss's house has everything one could need ... (*to herself*) except for love.

DON: But I left it right here, in the bushes behind the house.

EVELYN: There's no need for hiding.

DON: It isn't me who's hiding, it's—

EVELYN: It's me. I've been hiding all this time. Hiding in my lonely office, unable to see beyond my office door. Hiding in this big and empty house, when everything I need is elsewhere.

DON: (raising his voice in hopes that Block will hear and come) Yes, it's hiding in the bushes behind your house! Let him come out and see you!

EVELYN: (*amused*) Let him come in.

She opens the door. Don doesn't move.

EVELYN: Will I go in alone? Will I be left again to tell my woes to no one but myself?

DON: No! (*raising his voice again for Block to hear*) It's time! It's time!

Evelyn pulls him in through the door and closes it behind them.

---

scene 2

Block comes out from behind the house, wearing the moustache, zipping up his fly, and looking for Don. Now the lights go behind one of the house's windows to reveal the interior of a living room with a couch in the middle and a clock on the wall. The living room communicates on one side with the front door and on the other with the bedroom, which is still not visible. Evelyn and Don enter the living room.

EVELYN: Have a seat, at least.

DON: Thank you, but I won't be long.

EVELYN: That remains to be seen.

BLOCK: (*hearing them, speaking to himself*) Margins mother of profit, I've been betrayed! After my path to the top was already marked out. The first paving block—me—was ready to be laid!

Evelyn pulls Don down to the couch with her.

DON: Let me tell you why I've come.

EVELYN: Shhhh, there's no need.

DON: Your employees are—and one of them in particular is—very taken with you, and with how you've used your skills to make it to the top.

EVELYN: It's lonely at the top.

DON: But the top can come together with the bottom.

EVELYN: My office is a plush prison. My husband put me here, where I wouldn't mingle with the workers but wouldn't be respected by the execs. Now the love is gone, but the prison remains.

DON: There is another who would join you in your prison.

EVELYN: Why do we let promotions place bars between us? (*She moves closer to him on the couch.*)

DON: I have the key to unlock your prison door.

BLOCK: (*loudly, to Don*) Pssssst!

DON: (*remembering his mission*) But I've left it outside! (He starts to get up.)

EVELYN: (*pulling him back down*) I have your keys right here.

Block clears his throat, as loudly as he can.

EVELYN: Hear the bullfrog, calling to its mate!

DON: (*standing up and moving toward the window*) Let me see it.

EVELYN: (*standing and catching him*) The couch, it's too hard. Let's move somewhere softer. (*She pulls him toward the bedroom.*)

Block raps his knuckles loudly under the windowsill.

DON: Yes ... yes. Only give me a moment. This has been so much for me to take in. I'll be right there.

Evelyn goes into the bedroom. The lights remain off there. Only later in the play will we see that it contains a bed, a closet, and, in addition to the large window facing the audience, a second window facing stage right. The space behind this second window is concealed by the wall of the house. Don goes to the living room window and looks out.

BLOCK: What are you doing?

DON: I'm helping you. Everything is going according to plan.

BLOCK: What plan?

DON: The new plan. Remember what they say about the best-laid plans of mice and men?

BLOCK: You mean about the best-laid men forgetting plans?

DON: I mean about the best-planned lays. They go awry. Sometimes you have to improvise.

BLOCK: With mice and men?

DON: Just get in here.

Don helps Block climb up through the window. His blockhead bangs loudly against the windowsill.

EVELYN: (*from the bedroom*) Is everything all right?

DON: It was the bullfrog, come to croon under your window. (*then, to Block, whispering*) Now's your chance—get in there! (*He pushes Block into the bedroom.*)

In the dark bedroom we see neither Block nor Evelyn.

EVELYN: Let me run my fingers through your locks, so thick and ... flat? Ah, your body's been worn down by years of labor. Let me touch your face, so soft and boyish ... and cracked and rough? Ah, a proper worker, manly beyond his years! Let me feel your heart, though I know it beats unsteadily ... ah, but now it's constant, solid, and unbreakable! Here, touch mine, mine too is a worker's heart. I never lost it! I was promoted, but my heart still beats with those I left behind.

Allen Sacks, Evelyn's husband, appears stage right. He unlocks the front door and loudly closes it behind him. Don jumps out the living room window and runs off stage.

EVELYN: Ah! Quick!

BLOCK: What?

EVELYN: My husband!

BLOCK: Corpulent corporations! I hadn't thought of that!

Evelyn pushes Block out the bedroom window that faces stage right, and we hear her quickly making herself presentable before entering the living room. Block falls behind the house with a loud bang and clang, out of the audience's sight.

---

scene 3

For a time, the stage is silent. Then we hear clanging sounds as Block tries to raise himself up out of a pile of buckets and garden tools. More silence. Then:

JULIA SACKS: (*unseen*) Could you get off me?

BLOCK: (*also unseen*) Excellent question.

JULIA: Let me help.

More loud clanging. Blocks comes rolling into view on stage. He sits up, buttons up his shirt, and discreetly checks his fly. Julia rolls into view after him. She sits up and dusts herself off, then pulls out a joint and lights up. She offers it to Block.

BLOCK: No, thanks. Fire hazard. (*He points to his wooden head.*)

JULIA: (*after another drag*) Have I seen you before? Are you the one they say goes after all the ladies?

BLOCK: (*pulling off the moustache and stuffing it in his pocket*) Nah. You got me confused.

JULIA: It's all right. I'm not into moustaches. Looks like my mom isn't either?

BLOCK: Your mother?

JULIA: (*sighing*) The only one I got.

BLOCK: The Boss's daughter!

JULIA: (*shrugging*) Sure. So you're from the company?

BLOCK: Indeed, I am! And a mighty fine company it is that I have the honor of serving, and your mother has the honor of bossing! I wouldn't hesitate to call it the finest company I've ever kept, or been kept by!

JULIA: (*laughing*) That's good.

BLOCK: Yes, it's good.

JULIA: You sound just like them.

BLOCK: Who?

JULIA: My mom and dad.

BLOCK: Your father?

JULIA: My mom's boss.

BLOCK: (*speaking now to the audience*) By Boss, the boss has a boss! With one pair of boots you've just been kicked, and already another pair's waiting to be licked.

JULIA: (*nodding*) No doubt. Always telling us what to do. They're just so square.

BLOCK: Well I uh, you know I have been called square myself ...

EVELYN: (*from inside the house*) Julia!

JULIA: Aw, man ... (*She snuffs out the joint and hides it under a bucket for future use.*) Coming!

Block starts to leave.

JULIA: (*to Block*) Hey, nice smoking with you. See you at the company sometime?

BLOCK: (*saluting her, making a knocking sound as his hand hits his block head*) Yes ma'am!

Julia is amused. Block leaves. Julia hurries to the front door.

scene 4

Evelyn, Allen, and Julia Sacks are in the living room. Allen wears a three-piece suit as gray as his personality.

EVELYN: Are you ready for tonight?

JULIA: No.

ALLEN: We've gone to considerable trouble to set this up for you. His parents are busy people.

JULIA: I don't care about his parents.

EVELYN: But they're very well positioned. And Theodore will be starting college this year at Richford.

ALLEN: Not every boy can get into Richford.

EVELYN: Not every boy's parents donate so much to Richford.

JULIA: Let him find a girl at Richford.

EVELYN: Next year you could apply to Richford.

JULIA: Have you made your annual donation?

ALLEN: Have you been smoking?

EVELYN: You need to think of your future.

JULIA: You already make me work for you at the company.

ALLEN: It gives you experience.

EVELYN: And connections.

ALLEN: It'll be great on your college application.

JULIA: It'd be greater if you paid me.

ALLEN: We're investing in your future.

EVELYN: He's a really nice boy.

JULIA: Date him yourself then.

EVELYN: (*She seriously considers the proposition until Allen nudges her and snaps her out of it.*) Have you been smoking?

ALLEN: He'll be here any minute now.

Julia starts walking toward the front door.

ALLEN: Where are you going?

JULIA: I have work to do at the company.

EVELYN: We gave you the evening off.

JULIA: I'm taking it back on.

Julia leaves and goes back to her joint on the other side of the house.

---

scene 5

The workers enter, stage left, without Block, Don, or George. They sniff, are surprised by the smell of Julia's joint, but then knock on the front door.

EVELYN: He's here early!

ALLEN: Julia!

Evelyn goes to the door with an exaggerated smile, which disappears when she sees who is on the other side. Emma hands her a piece of paper.

EVELYN: What is this?

EMMA: A petition.

CARLA: We all signed it!

EMMA: Most of us. We couldn't find Block or Don. We didn't ask George ...

EVELYN: What do you mean "a petition"?

BENEDICT: I wasn't sure this would be the best ...

EVELYN: A petition for what?

EMMA: We're not happy about you making us work extra hours without warning.

CLIFFORD: If we're gonna spend so much time at work, I want a couch in the break room.

BENEDICT: I want more overtime.

EMMA: We're asking for more flexibility. If someone wants to work less and someone wants to work more ...

EVELYN: Then they can work somewhere else.

VICTORIA: Let's go. I knew she wouldn't read it.

EVELYN: Go. And never come back!

Evelyn slams the door. The workers look at one another, then leave.

---

scene 6

Theodore Dump enters with a large bouquet of roses. He sniffs, reacts with surprise to the smell of pot, but then shrugs and knocks at the door. Evelyn opens, angry, thinking the workers have come back.

EVELYN: Theodore! What a wonderful surprise!

THEODORE: You weren't expecting me?

EVELYN: Yes, of course. Come in. Sit down.

Theodore comes in and sits down.

ALLEN: Julia will be right here.

EVELYN: She's had to cancel your date. I'm so sorry. She came down with something.

ALLEN: Yes, she's right here, but she can't go out.

THEODORE: Can I give her my flowers?

ALLEN: It isn't pretty.

THEODORE: The bouquet?

EVELYN: We mean, you won't want to see her like this.

THEODORE: Then I'll just leave them here. (*He sets the flowers down on the table.*) I'll visit again when she's well.

ALLEN: Please do, as soon as possible.

THEODORE: Before I leave, I must pass my mother's regards on to you, Mr. Sacks.

ALLEN: (*embarrassed*) Thank you. Thank her. So thoughtful of our CEO to send her attentions all the way down here.

THEODORE: I should also pass my father's greetings on to the lady of the house.

EVELYN: (*likewise embarrassed*) Theodore, we've been keeping you too long.

Theodore nods goodbye and heads toward the door.

---

scene 7

Rearman enters stage left with a single, drooping flower picked from the side of the road. He waves off the smell of Julia's joint and knocks on the door. Theodore stops, having not yet left. Evelyn opens the door. Seeing Rearman, she blocks the doorway.

EVELYN: I told you to never to come back.

REARMAN: That was work. I'm not coming for work. I want to see Julia.

EVELYN: She isn't here.

THEODORE: She isn't?

EVELYN: She's sick.

REARMAN: So am I. Sick in love. Let me wish her well in our shared sickness.

EVELYN: She has a different sickness.

REARMAN: Let me breathe her infectious air. It is already she that ails me. I'll cherish her every microbe like a kiss.

EVELYN: You're worse than the workers. All they want to take over is the company.

REARMAN: (*as if snapping out of his lovesickness*) The workers? What? I'm away for a single day, and already they're out of line!

Julia finishes her joint and walks up behind Rearman as he speaks.

EVELYN: Julia! You shouldn't be going out in your condition. (*To Theodore*) She must have climbed out her bedroom window. (*to Julia*) Go back to your room right now.

REARMAN: (*going down on his knees and offering his flower, which now droops almost to the floor*) Julia! They cannot separate what is meant to be together! (*He bends, like his flower, to kiss the ground before her.*)

EVELYN: Your face and the ground?

In the meantime, Allen has picked up the bouquet of flowers that Theodore left on the table. He puts it back in Theodore's hands, then pulls Theodore toward Julia and stretches Theodore's arms, with the bouquet, in her direction. Julia now stands between two offerings of flowers. She leaves them both and begins to walk toward the door.

JULIA: Sorry guys. I already have a boyfriend.

EVELYN: What?

ALLEN: Since when?

JULIA: Since today.

REARMAN: Who?

JULIA: A worker from the company.

The curtain closes as the band strikes up "Mr. Block."

Act III.

Wednesday. At a diner across the street from the company premises.

scene 1

The curtain opens to reveal a quiet eatery, whose name, "Wine & Diner," appears in a big sign on the wall. The diner has two entrances, one on each side of the stage. The counter is in the back, with a door to the kitchen behind it. On the wall above the counter hangs a large clock. It's 8:30 am. At a table in one corner sits Aggie, disguised in a wig with thick glasses. At a table in another corner sits Rearman, quietly eating a slice of pie. Block is sitting at another table, stage center. A waitress approaches him.

WAITRESS: You sure you're in the right place? You've been waiting here since 6.

BLOCK: I'd rather be across the street at work, but the place doesn't open till 9!

WAITRESS: Do you want some coffee while you wait?

BLOCK: Nah. Just thinking about work warms me enough.

The waitress shrugs and leaves. Emma enters, orders something at the counter, and looks for a place to sit.

EMMA: Block, you made it! So she connected with you last night?

BLOCK: She did? I mean, yes, indeed! I mean, what?

EMMA: Carla was trying to reach you to tell you about our meeting. Anyway, you're here. The others should be coming soon.

BLOCK: Ah, an extra meeting. Work before work. I like it.

The waitress brings Emma a coffee. Carla arrives and orders something for herself at the counter.

EMMA: (*to Carla*) You have the petition?

Carla takes out the petition and lays it on the table.

BLOCK: A petition? What for?

EMMA: Better working conditions.

BLOCK: Better wor– now hold on there! Better wor– what? Better wor…

CARLA: –king conditions!

BLOCK: King conditions! Now that's something I can sign up for.

CARLA: Here. You're the only one who still hasn't signed!

BLOCK: If you all signed, then who'll be king?

EMMA: Block, we just need to think how to make our demands—

BLOCK: Demands? Now wait a minute. Let's not do anything rash. I'm allergic to rashes.

The waitress returns with a coffee for Carla. Don arrives—his moustache back in place—and whispers flirtatiously into the waitress's ear. The waitress rolls her eyes and leaves.

DON: (*to Block, lowering his voice*) Sorry to leave you in the lurch last night.

BLOCK: I wouldn't quite call her a …

EMMA: So, we decided to meet to talk about our demands.

The waitress comes with a glass of water for Don, which she deliberately spills in his lap. While Don jumps up, wincing from the cold, Victoria and Benedict arrive. Victoria goes to the counter to place her order, and Benedict snaps his fingers at the waitress, who ignores him.

EMMA: I think there are enough of us to get started. We have a lot to discuss.

The waitress brings a coffee for Victoria. Benedict snaps at her again, and she turns away.

CARLA: Shouldn't we wait for Aggie?

Aggie gets up then from her table in the corner. She lifts her wig and glasses just long enough for the others to recognize her, and she joins them at the table.

EMMA: So the boss refused to listen to—

Clifford arrives.

CLIFFORD: Whoa, hey guys! Wait ... oh, man, there was a meeting, wasn't there?

EMMA: Yes. Sit down.

CLIFFORD: (*sitting down*) I totally forgot ... I was just coming to hang out for a bit. Wait—you're not all planning on being at work at nine, are you?

EMMA: Look, we only have a few minutes now. What are we going to—

George arrives.

GEORGE: Hi everyone!

The others are silent.

GEORGE: What're you all doing here?

Silence.

GEORGE: What's wrong? I didn't mean to interrupt. Keep going.

Silence.

GEORGE: Here, I'll just pull up a chair and ...

He reaches for a chair from another table.

EMMA: George ... this meeting is only for workers.

GEORGE: What? I'm the foreman for one day and I'm already out of the loop? Did I change my old overalls? Did my PBRs ferment into IPAs? Did I start drinking my coffee with fancy foam? (*No one answers.*) Whatever. I've got work to do. (*turning toward the counter*) Gimme a cappuccino. To go.

George goes to the counter to wait for his cappuccino. The others watch him quietly until his cappuccino is ready. He takes it and leaves.

BENEDICT: I'm going too.

The waitress goes to the clock above the counter and, making loud ticking sounds, turns the hands to 8:55, gaining the workers' attention.

BLOCK: It is almost nine!

EMMA: Can we just quickly decide what—

Julia arrives. The workers watch her quietly as she orders a coffee at the counter. Then she turns toward them.

JULIA: Hi Block!

The workers turn to Block, surprised.

JULIA: Hi guys! (*She notices the petition on the table.*) Hey, are you all up to something? (*She pulls over a chair and sits down.*) Exciting!

Evelyn arrives.

JULIA: Quick! Before she sees you! I'll distract her.

Emma, Carla, Don, Benedict, Victoria, and Clifford leave through the door opposite Evelyn. (Emma drops some money for their bill on the table.) Aggie goes back to a corner table. Block gets up to leave after the others. Julia, noticing that they've left the petition on the table, picks it up, then embraces Block, holding the petition out of Evelyn's view while she shoves it into his back pocket. Just as Evelyn comes near and notices them, Julia gives Block a long, deep kiss. Evelyn stops, shocked. Rearman, still in the corner of the diner, stands up.

REARMAN: (*to the audience*) So he's the one! He won't be anymore, before this play is done!

scene 2

Julia releases Block from her embrace. Block is as shocked as Evelyn.

BLOCK: Ma'am, Boss, I ... was just on my way to work.

JULIA: Me too.

Block hurries out. Julia picks up her coffee at the counter and leaves with it, just behind Block. The waitress turns the clock to 9:00. Evelyn sits down, and Ronald Dump arrives. He almost looks like a regular guy, except that his tie appears to be made of dollars sewn together, and his suit is woven from silver thread. His hair-piece looks like it's woven from gold. He orders something at the counter, then sees Evelyn and sits down with her.

EVELYN: Ronald, I appreciate your coming all the way out here.

RONALD: The pleasure is mine, Evelyn. A CEO needs to spend some time near the hard-working Joes who keep this company running.

EVELYN: If we let them get too close, they'll have us on the run.

RONALD: That's why we have you between them and us. (*He pats her on the shoulder.*)

EVELYN: And what do we have you for?

RONALD: (*reaching his hand toward hers*) You have me for whatever you ...

The waitress arrives with two coffees and two omelets.

RONALD: (*eating heartily*) The people here! The salt of the earth!

EVELYN: It's the bacon you're tasting. Add some pepper.

RONALD: Evelyn, you're looking ... not quite as lovely today as usual.

EVELYN: It's Julia.

RONALD: No, it's you. Julia's even lovelier than her mother. Younger. (*He looks over Evelyn.*) Slimmer.

EVELYN: She's falling into bad company.

RONALD: Whose company?

EVELYN: A worker's.

RONALD: Could workers have their own company?

EVELYN: We need to help Theodore win her over.

RONALD: Theodore?

EVELYN: Your son.

RONALD: Ah, that one.

EVELYN: Why don't you give him some pointers?

RONALD: You know I'm an expert. It's in my genes. But somehow not in his genes. How do you figure that? Speaking of what's in my jeans ...

He clasps her hand. She shakes her hand free.

EVELYN: Never mind. I have a better idea.

RONALD: What?

He leans toward her. She gets up.

EVELYN: I have to go make a phone call. Tell Theodore to call me, too.

She leaves.

RONALD: (*standing up, not having finished his omelet*) This place is a dump. Next time I'll stay downtown.

Ronald leaves, ignoring the waitress as she gestures at his unpaid bill.

---

scene 3

The waitress turns the clock to 11:00. Rearman enters, places an order at the counter, and sits down.

REARMAN: Of course, the fool is late. Thinks he can throw around his new influence and make me wait. It doesn't matter. The price is small. I'll earn it back with interest when I see him fall. The stage is set. I'll just feed him the lines. He'll bite 'em, hook and sinker, and then Julia—and the job—are mine.

Block enters and joins Rearman at his table. The waitress brings two coffees. Block leaves his untouched.

REARMAN: Listen, Block, I know we've had our differences.

BLOCK: Yes. I want the foreman's job, but you want ...

REARMAN: Well, no, there we're the same.

BLOCK: I want to get in good with the boss, while you ...

REARMAN: OK, we're the same on that point too. What I'm trying to say is, let's let bygones be bygones.

BLOCK: The boss?

REARMAN: Maybe, soon enough, but let me cut to the chase. It's Julia I came to talk about. I want to help you.

BLOCK: Me too.

REARMAN: I know just how you can impress her.

BLOCK: Hard work.

REARMAN: God no! She hates work. But she loves workers. Pretends to, anyway. Does it to rebel against her parents.

BLOCK: Re– what?

REARMAN: –bel.

BLOCK: Bell! My favorite instrument! Rings when I wake up, rings when I start work.

REARMAN: You need to rile up the workers. Complain. Organize a strike. A work stoppage.

BLOCK: (*shocked*) A work st ... stop work?

REARMAN: I know, I know. You're an honest man. You'd never do a thing like that. It's like stabbing the bosses in the back. But this is for a higher cause. If you impress Julia, you impress the bosses. If you get in with her, you get in with them. Get it?

BLOCK: But what about you?

REARMAN: You don't need to impress me.

BLOCK: Right.

REARMAN: I'll just be happy to see you cause 'em some trouble, after what they did to me.

BLOCK: (*A bell goes off on Block's cell phone.*) Ah, listen to that!

Break's ending.

REARMAN: Sure, get back there before the boss starts suspecting something. But then get down to business, quick. That rich kid Theodore is hot on her tail. If you wait, she's his.

Block nods and leaves. Rearman finishes both coffees, pays, and leaves as well.

---

scene 4

The waitress turns the clock to 1:00. Theodore and Don enter the diner from opposite entrances.

DON: You must be Theodore.

THEODORE: (*nervous*) Don?

DON: Evelyn told me you needed help.

THEODORE: She really wants me to, well, but ...

DON: Theodore, leave the doubting to the girl. When you know you're good, you'll be the one to ease her doubts.

THEODORE: OK.

DON: Tell me something about her.

THEODORE: I hardly know her.

DON: The more the mystery. Now turn the tables. Become her mystery too. What doesn't she know about you?

THEODORE: Well ...

DON: Think of the wonders of female longing! She wants what she doesn't have, what will balance her. Be what she isn't.

THEODORE: She isn't a worker.

DON: I wouldn't wish that on anybody. Listen, let's go step by step.

Start by complimenting little things.

THEODORE: She has small ...

DON: The small but elegant choices she makes. How she's done her hair today. How she takes her coffee. Then you work your way up.

THEODORE: To her big ... ?

DON: Ideas, personality, precisely. I think we need to practice. (*Theodore nods.*) I'll play the girl, and you play you. (*Don takes off his moustache.*)

THEODORE: (*Looking into Don's eyes, he regains confidence.*) Hello.

DON: (*playing Julia*) Hi, Theodore.

THEODORE: Call me Theo. You look nice like this, clean shaven.

DON: Thank you, Theo. So do you.

THEODORE: I like this diner. Do you come here often?

DON: Every day. I don't see you here much.

THEODORE: That might change.

Julia enters and goes to the counter to order a coffee. At first Don and Theodore don't notice her.

DON: (*out of his Julia-character*) Now don't move too fast. But you're doing well. (*in character*) May I join you?

THEODORE: I was going to join you.

Julia, waiting for her coffee, listens in.

DON: Just for a bit.

THEODORE: It's so nice to talk to you.

Theodore reaches out and touches Don's hand. He slowly pulls Don toward him and is going to kiss him.

JULIA: (*to the audience*) So he's not interested in me after all! (*to them*) Hi guys.

Don and Theodore turn to her, startled.

JULIA: Sorry. Didn't mean to interrupt.

DON: (*whispering to Theodore*) Start again, but now with her!

THEODORE: (*unenthusiastic*) Hi Julia ... nice coffee.

JULIA: Thanks. You too. See you around.

Julia leaves with her coffee. Theodore puts some money on the table and leaves with Don

---

scene 5

The waitress turns the clock to 1:30. Allen and Block enter from opposite entrances.

ALLEN: Mr. Block?

BLOCK: Yes, sir!

They shake hands.

ALLEN: Have a seat.

Block sits down.

ALLEN: Have a drink?

BLOCK: No thanks. Seat's enough.

Allen places an order, then sits down with Block.

ALLEN: (*to Block*) Now listen to me, Block, there's something we need to discuss, tête à tête.

BLOCK: Tet-a-what?

ALLEN: Face to face.

BLOCK: Got it, teat to face.

ALLEN: My dear fellow, Mrs. Sacks tells me that ...

BLOCK: Mrs. Sacks? (*to the audience*) I've been found out! The game is up! (*to Allen*) Mrs. Sacks! Wonderful woman. Hardly know her. Quality boss is what I mean to say, that's her.

ALLEN: I have not come to speak of her. I've come to speak of our daughter.

BLOCK: (*to the audience*) Aha! The game has just begun!

The waitress brings Allen a scotch.

ALLEN: Mr. Block, it's come to my attention that you've been spending time with her.

BLOCK: And the very best of my time it is! Except for my time at work, of course.

ALLEN: Your work, indeed, that is just what I hoped to discuss with you.

BLOCK: Yes, sir!

ALLEN: My wife and I are concerned that our daughter has begun a relationship with a worker.

BLOCK: A what?

ALLEN: Mr. Block, don't be dense. (*Block runs his hand over his dense head.*) It isn't proper for a young lady with her prospects to be going around with an ordinary worker.

BLOCK: A worker? What worker? Tell me who he is!

ALLEN: Block!

BLOCK: Block? You mean? (*He looks around the room before looking back to himself.*) Me, a wor ... a work ... er ... a ... you got me all wrong!

ALLEN: You've just been going on about all your work.

BLOCK: And work I love! It's the –er that gives me trouble.

ALLEN: Well, it matters little what you call yourself. Julia has a palpable interest in you. And that interest is not in her interest.

BLOCK: Interesting ...

ALLEN: Julia has a successful life ahead of her. Surely you understand we don't want anything holding her down. We cannot allow just any worker ...

BLOCK: Ow!

ALLEN: Employee ...

BLOCK: Associate, partner, team member!

ALLEN: Oh, dear, do you mean to say you actually believe us when we call you that? Please, let us be reasonable. I simply cannot imagine how it could work out.

BLOCK: I'll work out and in.

ALLEN: You come from thoroughly divergent backgrounds. You see things differently.

BLOCK: I always see things from the perspective of the bosses.

ALLEN: Yet what will happen if the workers ...

BLOCK: Eeeeah!

ALLEN: ... if the team members begin demanding higher pay, petitioning, even organizing a strike? Would you date a woman who's on the other side when you picket?

BLOCK: Pick what?

ALLEN: Picket lines.

BLOCK: I'd pick her is what I'd pick. Her and her company. Strike and all.

ALLEN: Strike and all?

BLOCK: (*to the audience*) Now I see what Rearman meant. This striking business might be Boss-sent! (*to Allen*) I'd strike a blow for the company, that's what I'd strike.

ALLEN: You'd strike for the company? Set a trap? Unveil the agitators with a fabricated strike?

BLOCK: Whatever we're in the business of fabricating.

ALLEN: You're serious?

BLOCK: Serious, by Boss, have I ever been funny?

ALLEN: Seriously, you wouldn't want shorter hours?

BLOCK: All my clocks are set to the long ones.

ALLEN: Higher pay?

BLOCK: Only a higher position.

ALLEN: We can discuss that, if you keep up the good attitude.

BLOCK: Yes, sir!

ALLEN: I'll approve of your relationship with Julia. For now.

Allen finishes his scotch. He pays. Both leave.

---

scene 6

The waitress turns the clock to 3:00. Evelyn Sacks and Don enter from opposite entrances and sit down together.

DON: Theodore's hopeless, Ev, with women.

EVELYN: So what do we do?

DON: Should I take on the task myself?

EVELYN: And waste your talents on so thankless a target? I'll think of something else.

Don leaves. Evelyn takes out her cell phone and makes a call.

EVELYN: Ronald, I have a favor to ask you ... I know an unmarried man would've been more suitable ... maybe someone a little more handsome ... but the urgency of the situation ... yes, Julia ...

Allen enters.

ALLEN: Evelyn!

EVELYN: (*to Ronald, on the phone*) I gotta go. (*She hangs up and turns to Allen.*) Everything's fine.

ALLEN: Everything's fine!

EVELYN: It is?

ALLEN: Mr. Block is a perfectly up-thinking, right-standing, good-attituded fellow.

EVELYN: He's a worker.

ALLEN: Yes, but don't tell that to him. He doesn't know it.

EVELYN: If I ever catch him causing trouble, I'll tear more than our daughter off him.

They leave.

scene 7

The waitress turns the clock to 5:00. Rearman arrives and sits inconspicuously at a table near the edge of the stage. After him, the workers arrive: Emma, Carla, Clifford, Benedict, Victoria, Don, and Block. As the scene unfolds, the waitress comes, takes their orders, and brings them coffee without interrupting the dialogue.

Their interactions with her are inaudible to the audience.

EMMA: So we didn't finish discussing in the morning. The boss rejected our petition.

BENEDICT: It was a bad petition.

CLIFFORD: We just need the boss to chill.

CARLA: We need to be strong! A show of force!

BENEDICT: We need a carefully worded statement.

DON: We need to say it with passion.

EMMA: We need someone to write it.

Silence. Emma looks around, and each of the others in turn hides her or his face, turns away, makes an apologetic shrug, or whistles in feigned indifference.

BLOCK: (*to the audience*) What have I gotten myself into? These folks are mad. Or they've been had. Confused. Bamboozed. A petition? Statement? Show of force? Just thinking of it makes my brain get hoarse. (*He pauses to think.*) Well, there could be reason in it. But where would you begin it? No, this must be crazy talk, or my name isn't ...

Before Emma's gaze reaches Block, Julia enters.

JULIA: Block! I'm glad I found you. And all of you. This company is killing me. What are we going to do?

She comes to them, pulls up a chair, and sits down beside Block. Block looks around uncomfortably and notices Rearman in the corner. Rearman points to Julia and smiles suggestively.

BLOCK: (*still to the audience*) But then, what Rearman said is also true ... (*He reaches into his back pocket and pulls out the petition.*)

JULIA: I can't take it anymore. They've been making me work here every day since summer started.

BENEDICT: Tough, isn't it, working for a whole month of your life?

BLOCK: Now come on, everywork has to start sometime.

JULIA: The conditions are unbearable.

VICTORIA: Did they lower your allowance?

BLOCK: Now what's this, folks? Are we not all associates here? Did we come here to fight among ourselves? (*Block pauses and looks toward Rearman, who nods at him encouragingly.*) Now you might say I have a block for a head, but I've still got eyes for eyes, and I look at this girl, and I can see, and you can see too, just look at her: is she the boss?

DON: Not at all. Evelyn's a bit finer in the cheeks, darker in the eyes ...

BLOCK: Bigger in the office, that's what Mrs. Sacks is. Listen now. No one respects a boss like I do, sure. But if you want to move up in the world, you've got to make your move. You've got to put your best boot forward, and then the other one too, and then your body over it, or you'll fall down. And don't trip up. Get going. Don't just knock on wood, knock with wood. Get all your hard knocks out of you and then knock harder! You can stick together or stick apart for all I care, but the sticks are less important than the branches and the trunk, and that's where I say we've got to be.

VICTORIA: Up a tree?

BLOCK: Up a tree or a ladder, doesn't matter. But up! Get up!

DON: (*getting up*) I'm up.

BLOCK: Get up!

CARLA: (*getting up*) OK!

BLOCK: Get up!

Emma, Clifford, and Julia stand up.

BLOCK: Get up!

Victoria and Benedict stand up, more reluctantly.

BLOCK: We're up!

EMMA: What now?

DON: I think Block just volunteered to write our statement.

BLOCK: Well, I ... (*He looks at Rearman, then at Julia. Julia looks back at him admiringly.*) Yes indeed, by Boss, I will.

EMMA: That's great. Let's talk about what should be in it.

CLIFFORD: Sorry to interrupt, but we agreed this meeting would be limited to ten minutes.

VICTORIA: Do you have some place to be?

CLIFFORD: I need to go hang out in the diner.

VICTORIA: Which diner?

CLIFFORD: This diner, after the meeting. I don't want to be late. Do you want to join me?

EMMA: Let's just take one minute to come up with a clear list of demands.

CLIFFORD: Block can take care of it.

BENEDICT: Can't do worse than the rest of you. Let's go.

Clifford walks to another table, sits down, and kicks up his legs to relax. Victoria watches him for a moment, considering his offer to hang out, but then she turns and leaves with Benedict, Carla, and Don. Clifford, finding himself alone at his table, pulls up the hood of his sweatshirt, leans back, and nods off. Julia comes to Block and gives him a pat on the back before leading him out. Emma tries in vain to get them all to stay. Aggie comes out from the door to the kitchen and finds only Emma at the meeting place.

AGGIE: Done already? How'd it go?

EMMA: We'll find out.

Aggie and Emma leave. Rearman remains at his table.

scene 8

The waitress turns the clock to 5:45. Evelyn enters and joins Rearman. Clifford is still asleep.

EVELYN: Tell me you're not wasting my time.

REARMAN: No, but Block is. More than that. He's been agitating the workers.

EVELYN: The son of a beech.

REARMAN: My thoughts exactly.

EVELYN: The daughter stealer.

REARMAN: It's serious.

EVELYN: The motherf—

REARMAN: I wouldn't go that far.

EVELYN: What are we going to do?

REARMAN: I recommend immediate termination and separation from Miss Sacks.

EVELYN: No. We'll act like we know nothing. Keep watching him. Let him lead you to them. When the moment is right, we strike.

REARMAN: As long as we do before they do.

Evelyn leaves. Rearman goes back to sit in his corner.

scene 9

The waitress turns the clock to 6:00. Block enters and sits down. He takes out a pen and the petition, which he turns over to write on the blank side. He writes down a few words, rereads them, shakes his head, and crosses them out. He writes and then erases another line. But when he writes a third line, he looks at it and smiles. He picks up his pen again and hurriedly fills the page. As he puts the finishing touches on the statement, Emma arrives. Rearman, seeing Block finish the statement, hurries away.

EMMA: Hi Block.

BLOCK: You're right on time. I just finished, and it's a beaut. The ideal workplace, that's what it shows!

He hands her the paper. Before Emma gets to read it, Carla arrives.

CARLA: It's all ready? Let me see!

Emma, still not having read the statement, hands it to Carla. Before Carla reads it, Don arrives.

DON: Afternoon ladies, Block. Let's see if this statement is as nice and strong as all of you.

Carla, still not having read the statement, hands it to Don. Before Don reads it, Victoria and Benedict arrive.

BENEDICT: How bad is it? Give it here.

Don, not having read the statement, hands it to Benedict and Victoria, who spend a moment passing it between one another. Still not having read it, they drop it on the table and sit down. The clanging of their moving chairs awakens Clifford at his table.

CLIFFORD: Oh, man, another meeting? I was just starting to get comfortable over here. (*He slowly gets up and joins them.*)

EMMA: Now that we're all here ...

Clifford has picked up the statement and is about to read it when Evelyn enters, led by Rearman. The others see her and watch her approach. Emma, whose back is turned to her, keeps speaking.

EMMA: ... we really should go over the points and agree on them before we show them to the boss.

The others, still watching Evelyn, don't respond.

EMMA: Maybe you're right. We should wait for Aggie and go over it with her. She has some experience in these things.

The others are still silent.

BLOCK: Oh, Boss.

EVELYN: You have something to show me?

EMMA: (*turning toward her*) Ah ...

BENEDICT: Nothing at all.

CLIFFORD: Whatever, let her deal with it.

CARLA: Well ...

VICTORIA: (*frowning*) Get it over with.

EMMA: Not yet ...

BLOCK: Here it is!

He hands her the statement. Evelyn reads the title.

EVELYN: "Statement of demands," eh? "For a better workplace"?

BLOCK: Yes, Boss!

EVELYN: Get out!

Nervous silence. Then Clifford shrugs and speaks.

CLIFFORD: It got a lot less pleasant here anyway since you came around.

He leaves. The others follow. Block lags behind the rest, looking at Rearman, who sneers at him. Then Block leaves too, head hanging low.

---

scene 10

The waitress turns the clock to 6:15. Evelyn sits down to read the statement.

EVELYN: (*to Rearman*) Get me a shot of something.

Rearman goes to the bar and orders something for her. While the waitress prepares it, Evelyn reads the statement. Her face gradually softens. Her fury subsides. Soon she's beaming.

EVELYN: Rearman, go find Block.

Rearman downs the shot he's ordered for Evelyn, then leaves. In a moment he returns with Block, who must have been waiting right outside.

EVELYN: I've got to hand it to you, Block.

Block reaches out to take something to be handed to him. Evelyn doesn't react.

EVELYN: I underestimated you.

BLOCK: Happens all the time.

EVELYN: I really believed you'd gone over to the agitators. But all along you'd been working for the company's good. Look at these demands. Brilliant.

Rearman orders himself another shot and downs it.

EVELYN: "A forty-hour workday."

BLOCK: Rearman told me to ask for a four-hour day, but that must've been a mistake.

EVELYN: "Lower pay."

BLOCK: Rearman told me to write "higher," but then how could the company afford the longer hours?

EVELYN: "No unions."

BLOCK: So that nothing comes between us.

EVELYN: And this is good: "a portrait of the boss in every room"!

BLOCK: Two in every room might get distracting.

Ronald arrives.

RONALD: Here I am, sugar-money. You look tremendous. Where's Julia? I'm ready for all your needs, especially hers.

EVELYN: Thank you, Ronald, but it won't be necessary anymore. We've just found her the perfect suitor.

She points to Block. Rearman takes the half-full bottle from the waitress and drinks straight from it, spilling most of it over his face.

RONALD: (*looking at Block*) This? Him? So sad. Wonderful. Looks fake, though. Is he real? (*He touches Block's head.*) Good. Just remember I'd do anything for you, Evelyn.

EVELYN: I want a promotion.

RONALD: Within reason, of course.

EVELYN: For putting down an organizing drive, I deserve a promotion.

As Ronald considers his reply, Julia enters.

JULIA: Hi Mom. You wanted me to meet someone?

Julia looks at Ronald, who struts toward her confidently, chest puffed out. But Evelyn points to Block.

JULIA: I know him already.

EVELYN: Right. But he looks so different now. (*to Block*) Did you used to wear a moustache?

BLOCK: Well ...

EVELYN: No, it's the aura of a man who's just screwed over his fellow workers. I recognize it anywhere.

RONALD: Thank you.

JULIA: Screwed over the workers?

Allen Sacks enters with Smelania Dump. Her outfit shows impeccable good taste, if you have a taste for wealth. The two of them coo and giggle with each other until they see Evelyn and Ronald.

EVELYN: Allen, I'm glad you're here.

ALLEN: (*looking at Ronald*) You are?

EVELYN: I'd like to introduce you to Mr. Block, our future son-in-law.

JULIA: What?

RONALD: Smelania, I am so happy to see you.

SMELANIA: (*looking at Evelyn*) I'm sure.

RONALD: I need to ask for a promotion.

SMELANIA: You're already CEO.

RONALD: But I have to promote Allen to CEO. He's the best. Except for me. And maybe you. But third or fourth best, maybe.

SMELANIA: Well ...

RONALD: Because Allen has to promote Evelyn to Allen's position as corporate managing director. She'll be perfect for the job. The best. Except for Allen. And me. And maybe you.

SMELANIA: Is that really necessary?

RONALD: Because Evelyn needs to promote Mr ... what's his ... ?

BLOCK: Block.

RONALD: Like I said, to be the local branch boss.

SMELANIA: I see.

RONALD: He's not the best by a long shot. Below average, really. But he just killed a union drive.

JULIA: Block, what's going on? It can't be what it looks like ...

Block whistles to himself, pretending not to hear her.

SMELANIA: I'll call Mr. Moffat right away to get the board's approval.

EVELYN: And now we can welcome Mr. Block into our great and intermingled houses—from now on family and finance, pleasure and profit, love and lucre, all will be one!

Julia stares, speechless. Rearman faints. The waitress comes back, sees them, and turns out the lights. The curtain closes as the band plays "Mr. Block."

Intermission

When the audience leaves the auditorium, entertainments begin in the halls outside, which have been gaudily decorated. The waitress from Act III joins the staff distributing refreshments. The band, having moved from the auditorium to the hall, once again strikes up the tune of "Mr. Block," this time with vocals:

BAND LEADER: What a way to end the play! Let's give it up for Mr. Block! Everybody, sing along!

He holds up the program, pointing to the song lyrics on the back. But it doesn't matter if the audience doesn't join in. The band leader prefers to sing alone.

Please give me your attention, I'll introduce to you
A man who is a credit to "Our Red, White, and Blue";
His head is made of lumber; he bears it like a cross;
He used to be a common worker. Now he is the boss!
And you can bet he may
Be CEO someday.

(*chorus*)

Oh, Mr. Block, you were born to be great!
A girl's perfect mate!
Fame and fortune await!
Set your clock, tick and tock, till we all rise and say:
You're the best boss in every way!

The song ends.

BAND LEADER: Now here's another one.

The band performs the following version of the "Wobbly Doxology" (to words that are, again, given on the back of the program).

Praise Block when tomorrow's work bells chime!
Praise him with labor's love sublime!
He slept his way to a higher class.
You working folks can kiss his ... sass!
Aw yeah.

Evelyn, Allen, Ronald, and Smelania arrive at the celebration and mingle with the attendees, shaking hands, praising their good taste in theater, recommending the best boss-themed mixed drinks at the bar, and thanking them for coming to celebrate Block's appointment, or embossment, if you will. Rearman, on orders from Evelyn, sullenly hands out invitations to the upcoming wedding reception of Mr. Block and Miss Julia Sacks, scheduled for Friday.

BAND LEADER: Just one more song. This one's been requested by someone in the audience. With feeling now!

to the tune of "Solidarity Forever"

When the boss's aspirations in the worker's head do stick,
They will make of him a blockhead, and he'll make his fellows sick.
He licked boots to make his way up, now it's his turn to be licked!
The boss gets marched upon!

Strong disparity forever, strong disparity forever,
Strong disparity forever, if the boss goes marching on!

Is there aught he holds in common with the average working schmucks
Who get paid a tiny pittance though we work from dawn to dusk?
Is there anything left for us but to tell him, "What the—"

Evelyn, belatedly paying attention to the words, interrupts, taking the band leader's mic and putting her free arm around Block.

EVELYN: Let me say a few words. Being boss takes someone tough as oak, someone hard-headed, someone hard all around, someone who gives in to no one, except his own boss, someone who never takes no for an answer because he never takes anything for a question. That man is right here. He's solid as a trunk, and I can't think of anyone better to hold up this branch while the whole company grows.

Allen, Ronald, and Smelania applaud. Evelyn gives Block the mic, but before he gets to speak, Aggie arrives, wearing her Joe Hill outfit again.

AGGIE: Block! Sorry I'm late. I was busy on another campaign. Have you already handed over the demands?

EVELYN: Who's this?

BLOCK: By Boss, I mean, by Me, I mean, oh my, don't worry, she's just ...

AGGIE: Block, what is this? Why are you standing up there with the boss? What did she say to your demands?

BLOCK: She said, he said ... let me just say, well now, let me answer with a demand of my own. I demand that you all have fun and enjoy this celebration. And quickly now, because we need to wrap this play up. Tomorrow we go back to work, bright and early!

Aggie turns to the crowd now and speaks to directly to them.

AGGIE: "Celebrate," he says! Party short and quick, then back to work!

BLOCK: Thank you, miss! Let's end on that high note. Exit's this way. (*He points.*)

Aggie goes to block the exit before anyone leaves. She pulls over a chair and stands on it.

AGGIE: "Let's end," he says! Well now, did you like the show? Is that the ending you came here wanting to see? "It's over," they always say—as soon as they've won! Go on. Leave, and that's the ending you get. It's over as long as you believe 'em when they say it's over. Trouble is, even after it's over and they've won, you've got to keep on living. And working. Are you going back to work tomorrow? You? You?

Aggie addresses her questions to the gathered crowd, which includes the theater staff as well as the audience. As they respond, Evelyn, Allen, Ronald, and Smelania try to silence Aggie. The waitress from Act III defends Aggie, blocking them so she can go on speaking.

AGGIE: The bosses want you to think this is their play, they're the actors, the world is their stage, and you're nothing but spectators looking on. You just came for a little entertainment, to stop thinking of your troubles for a while. They want you to watch their spectacle until they tell you it's over and it's time to go home. Did you have fun? Are you going home like that, like all's well that's ended well? Or will you keep on fighting tomorrow at work like it isn't over, because the play goes on, there's another act, the end is only an intermission, because on the stage of the world there's just one long play, and we're all actors in it, and we're not going to let them tell us when ...

Rearman rushes toward her and tries to cover her mouth with his hand. Evelyn motions for the band to start playing again. But just as the band begins to strike up "Mr. Block," the workers burst into the hall. Victoria and Benedict hang back near the exit, a bit uncomfortable, while Emma, Carla, Clifford, and Don hand out folded sheets of paper containing the new words to "Solidarity Forever" sung earlier by the band, and the original lyrics to "Mr. Block," as written by Joe Hill, which the workers start singing as the band plays.

Oh, Mr. Block, you were born by mistake,
You take the cake,
You make me ache.
Tie on a rock to your block and then jump in the lake,

Kindly do that for Liberty's sake.

During the song, Aggie wrests herself free of Rearman and encourages the audience to sing along. The workers, now helped by the theater staff, continue handing out the folded song sheets, which open up to reveal a new program for the play. Unlike the program distributed earlier, which mentioned only Acts I to III, this one also lists Acts IV and V. Here, the title is given as Reappraise Boss! and the description reads "A proletarian sex tragicomedy in five acts (a tragedy for Mr. Block, a comedy for the working class!)" The sheet is also covered with slogans like "Labor's Love's Lost!" "New boss, spelled with the same BS!" and "Take a chip off the new Block!" The last page of the folded paper contains a "Postscript" to the play. (See below.) When the song is over, Emma takes the mic.

EMMA: Block's just barely started being boss, and things are even worse than before.

CLIFFORD: (*taking the mic*) I asked Block for time off work to come to this party. So he gave me a tray to work here as a waiter for the bosses!

CARLA: (*taking the mic*) I asked for time off to play in the fourth and fifth acts, and Block told me the play was over!

THE WORKERS: (*shouting and encouraging the audience to join in*) Fourth and fifth! Fourth and fifth!

BLOCK: Now calm down everyone. There's been a misunderstanding's all there's been. I just meant to say that all the narrative's been tied up, you know, problems solved, the hero achieved his goal, Mr. Block's hard work earned its fair reward. But of course you paid for a full evening of entertainment, and the bosses would never cheat you of entertainment, no way. Just think what might happen if people stopped being entertained! Come back into the auditorium now for another dose of happy lyric before the night is through.

The audience follows Block back into the auditorium. Block climbs on stage and begins to sing (without the support of the band) the celebratory version of "Mr. Block" ("Oh, Mr. Block, you were born to be great ..."). But he stops when he sees the workers begin setting the stage for Act IV. Block tries to stop them, pushing pieces of the set away, but they work too fast for him, and he gives up. He starts singing to the tune of "Solidarity Forever": "Mr. Block will rule forever! ... Mr. Block goes marching on!" but finally he realizes he can't stop Act IV from coming. He sits down on a chair that's been brought in as part of the new set. The lights go out.

Act IV.

Thursday. At the new boss's house.

scene 1

When the stage lights turn back on, we see a set identical to that of the boss's house from Act II. This time the bedroom lights are on, and we see a large closet behind a large bed. Over the bed hangs a picture, perhaps an equestrian portrait of XYZ owner and board chair Florian Moffat setting out to rescue his employees from the immorality of sloth, or maybe just a still-life of a dollar bill. In the living room sits Mr. Block, wearing a new suit, alone. The house, as we soon learn, is his. He gets up from his chair and walks about, marveling at the clean, shiny surfaces and luxurious amenities.

BLOCK: A bed and a couch—we bosses know how to live! Accumulating capitalists! What more could life give? A stainless carpet. Clean, white walls. (*He tests the lights.*) I have seen the light, and it works, every bulb!

He is still venerating the fully functional chandelier when Rearman enters stage left and rings the doorbell. Block collects himself and opens the door.

REARMAN: (*with feigned warmth*) Mr. Block, let me compliment you on a fine celebration last night.

BLOCK: Thank y–

REARMAN: I'll be quick. I want to help you.

BLOCK: Me too.

REARMAN: The company needs a union buster.

BLOCK: A who-nion buster?

REARMAN: Listen, Block, I know they're only workers. But if they get together, do you realize how dangerous they can be?

BLOCK: No.

REARMAN: Then it'll be my job to make sure they don't realize either.

BLOCK: Realize what?

REARMAN: See how good I am at it.

BLOCK: Rearman, I owe you one for helping me get promoted. You're hired.

REARMAN: I'll help you take the next step off the corporate ladder. Just wait!

BLOCK: Up the corporate ladder!

Rearman shrugs. Don enters stage left and rings the doorbell.

REARMAN: I'd better get to work! You just take it easy. I'll have it all under control.

---

scene 2

Rearman opens the door and leaves, scowling at Don.

BLOCK: Divine dividends, Don, I forgot you were coming!

Don comes in.

DON: I still am a little upset about that incident with writing up our demands. But friends are friends, right? So you're looking to turn up the charm on Julia?

BLOCK: Considering how the charm has already turned, and recalibrating the gauge on my heartstrings, I was hoping ... you see ... It's the boss, I mean Corporate Managing Director Evelyn, that I yearn for now. Again. I love her like flowers and honey.

DON: Flowers and honey?

BLOCK: Pardon, love is clouding my speech. I mean like power and money.

DON: And Julia?

BLOCK: Does she love power and money too?

DON: It's not my business to pry. I support all love, however base.

BLOCK: Second base might be enough for another promotion, but if I have to go all the way, so be it.

DON: Let's not get ahead of ourselves. Where we were last time we met?

BLOCK: You were shoving me into the boss's bedroom.

DON: Before that. Think about making pleasant conversation. Find something you have in common. Go with that. But don't go overboard.

BLOCK: (*pointing to his wooden head*) I'm generally under board.

DON: Don't let your kindness smother her.

BLOCK: Don't s'mother the one, don't s'daughter the other ...

JULIA: (*entering stage left and calling from outside the house*) Hey Block, it's me!

DON: (*hurriedly*) Practice on her, at least.

Don runs into the bedroom, looks around, and goes to hide in the closet. Julia lets herself in.

BLOCK: Julia! It's all right to see you ...

JULIA: I need to talk to my mother. Have you seen her?

BLOCK: Not yet.

JULIA: Speaking of not seeing things, I think you should get down to the company. The workers aren't too happy with your new policies.

BLOCK: What policies?

JULIA: Rearman just announced them for you. Maybe you should go and sort things out.

BLOCK: Don't worry. Rearman has it under control.

JULIA: (*after a pause*) Block, tell me you know what you're doing.

BLOCK: I've never known anything else.

JULIA: Like, you're just fooling them, right, pretending to be on the company's side? I know you still have something up your sleeve … right?

BLOCK: (*examining his sleeves*) My own muscles. Hard as my head. And smarter too.

JULIA: (*Laughing, she gives him an affectionate punch in the arm.*) Well, they deserve whatever you've got planned for 'em.

She leaves.

scene 3

Allen Sacks enters stage left and rings the doorbell. Block lets him in.

ALLEN: Mr. Block! Have you seen my dear daughter?

BLOCK: You just missed her, Mister.

ALLEN: I need to have a talk with that poor girl. Dispel some misinformation.

BLOCK: How d'ya spell it? Miss who?

ALLEN: No matter. I also wanted to come, without delay, to congratulate you.

BLOCK: I owe it all to you.

ALLEN: You earned this promotion yourself, Mr. Block.

BLOCK: I mean the loan you made me so I could buy this house. I owe it all to you.

ALLEN: Think nothing of it. The favor will be easily repaid.

BLOCK: I hadn't even thought of repaying. (*a pause*) Speaking of paying, I'd better get to work.

ALLEN: Certainly. I'll look after the house while you're gone.

BLOCK: Why, thank you, boss. (*to the audience*) The ways of the wealthy are strange for sure. Such generosity! I've got something to learn.

Smelania enters stage left and rings the doorbell.

ALLEN: I'll get that. (*He opens.*) Welcome, my dear, let me show you around.

BLOCK: Yes, let me—

ALLEN: Not necessary. We would hate to take up any more of your time.

BLOCK: (*nonetheless attempting to show them around*) This way is the kitchen. Here is the bathroom ...

Allen and Smelania go straight toward the bedroom. They open the door and enter. While still in the doorway, Allen turns back to Block.

ALLEN: Oh, and Block, if you see Mr. Moffat, be a dear and don't mention we were here.

He winks at Block and shuts the door. As Allen and Smelania embrace in the bedroom, Block turns to leave. But before he reaches the door, Evelyn enters stage left and rings the doorbell.

scene 4

Block opens and sees Evelyn.

BLOCK: (*speaking loudly, so that his voice carries into the bedroom*) Corporate Managing Director Sacks! Mergers Mother of Money, Evelyn, I wasn't expecting you!

When Allen and Smelania hear Block, Allen jumps out the nearest window and runs away, while Smelania hides herself in the closet. Block momentarily turns away from Evelyn, takes a marker out of his pocket, and draws an elegant moustache on his face.

BLOCK: (*turning back to Evelyn*) It's so nice to see you. (*seductively*) Can I get you a drink of water?

EVELYN: (*ignoring his offer*) Have you seen Julia?

BLOCK: I have been seeing her, yes, but that doesn't mean that you and I can't ...

EVELYN: They said at the office she was looking for me.

BLOCK: She was just here. Why don't you stay a while and wait?

She sits down on the couch.

EVELYN: Nice house. (*She looks around the room, which, as we said, is exactly like her own living room.*) You're really making a name for yourself, you know.

BLOCK: (*embarrassed*) I try to live up to it.

EVELYN: It suits you, the suit. On those broad, square shoulders. It's like you're a changed man since we first met.

BLOCK: You could change me even more.

EVELYN: Your positive attitude is getting you noticed all the way at the top.

BLOCK: I have a positive attitude toward the top, but a negative attitude toward the bottom.

EVELYN: Does that attitude extend to all bottoms?

BLOCK: I still look up to the bottom of the top.

EVELYN: (*pulling Block toward her on the couch*) Keep looking up, Block. One never knows when a top might come off.

BLOCK: Oh, Boss, you don't know how much I want you from top to bottom, but I'm not sure this is the place.

EVELYN: No, this isn't.

She stands up and tries to pull him to the bedroom.

BLOCK: Wait! There's someone, I mean something, I mean, sham it to sell! I ...

EVELYN: You're right. I was carried away.

BLOCK: (*moving toward her*) No, I'll carry you away!

EVELYN: (*moving toward Block*) Block!

Ronald enters stage left.

RONALD: (*ringing the doorbell*) Block!

BLOCK: I've been blocked.

Block and Evelyn compose themselves. Block opens the door.

RONALD: (*heartily embracing Block*) Look at you, a wonderful boss. The best. Well, not bad. 7 out of 10. Maybe 5. Here. (*Gives Block a coin.*) Give yourself a little waxing for me. (*looks around*) My, my, maybe it's the house that makes the man. Am I glad I made that loan to Allen who made the loan to you!

BLOCK: You're glad?

RONALD: The house might come in handy. (*He looks around and pretends just to notice Evelyn.*) Evelyn! You look marvelous. At least compared to this guy here. Look at those two faces. Show me around.

BLOCK: Here is the kitchen ...

Ronald takes Evelyn by the hand and pulls her toward the bedroom. Before Block can block their way, Ronald opens the door and pushes Evelyn in. He turns back and tosses Block another coin. It bounces off Block's head and lands on the floor.

BLOCK: Now wait a minute, maybe Corporate Managing Evelyn didn't—

RONALD: (*shushing him*) If you see Mr. Moffat, you didn't see me here.

He closes the bedroom door. Block rubs the moustache off his face.

---

scene 5

Allen enters stage left and rings the doorbell. Block opens the door.

BLOCK: (*surprised to see Allen, whom he last saw entering the bedroom*) CEO Sacks!

When Evelyn and Ronald hear him, Evelyn jumps out the window and Ronald goes to hide in the closet.

BLOCK: You ...

ALLEN: Have had a nice cool shower and a fine brisk walk. A thousand thanks to you, dear sir, I mean servant, for providing comfort and refuge to a poor superior in the hour, or shall I say minute, of his need.

BLOCK: Think nothing of it.

ALLEN: I do. Listen, Mr. Block, I come bearing a message for you, straight from the top. XYZ Group would like to offer you a promotion.

BLOCK: But I ...

ALLEN: No buts.

BLOCK: Then ...

ALLEN: We're offering you the position of Corporate Managing Director downtown.

BLOCK: But that's Boss Sacks's job!

ALLEN: Fear not. We have other plans for my dear wife. You are the focus of our company's attentions at present.

Evelyn, having walked around the house, rings the doorbell. Block opens for her.

BLOCK: Corporate Managing ... Evelyn! (*He looks at her, then at the bedroom, then back at her.*)

EVELYN: Allen! I didn't expect to see you here.

BLOCK: Here, let me show you around.

He leads them straight to the bedroom, pushes them in, and closes the door behind them.

---

scene 6

George enters stage left and rings the doorbell. Block opens.

GEORGE: There's a problem.

BLOCK: Just don't go in the bedroom and you'll be fine.

GEORGE: It's at the company. The workers are really upset about the new conditions.

BLOCK: What new conditions?

GEORGE: Rearman took away all their breaks. He said he did it on your behalf.

BLOCK: If it was for the good of the company, then he did it on my be-whole.

GEORGE: If it makes them stop working, is that good for the company?

BLOCK: What are you saying?

GEORGE: I'm just not sure that Rearman has a knack for ... people.

BLOCK: That's all right. He won't be at the job for long.

GEORGE: Aha. That might be ... wise. But I really think you should come over and sort things out yourself.

BLOCK: I'm no longer the local boss. I've been promoted to Corporate Managing Director downtown.

GEORGE: And you're looking for someone to take your place?

BLOCK: (*touching George on the shoulder*) I've already found him.

GEORGE: (*excited*) Yeah?

BLOCK: Rearman!

GEORGE: What? Are you sure that's ... ?

Julia enters stage left and enters the house without ringing.

GEORGE: I'll try to calm things down there while we wait for you. (*He leaves.*)

JULIA: I heard my mom came this way. I need to talk to her.

BLOCK: (*looking toward the bedroom*) She should be here any minute now. I doubt they'll last long.

JULIA: It's about my dad. He's been talking to Smelania Dump. You know, the CEO of XYZ Group.

BLOCK: Not only talking.

JULIA: They're trying to force my mom out of the company. He used her to get where he is, and now he wants her out of the way.

BLOCK: He used her?

JULIA: He only got his job thanks to her. She was already forewoman when they met. She gave him a job here, and he licked his bootstraps right past her up the corporate ladder.

Block gestures with his hands and face as he tries to envision Julia's metaphor.

JULIA: She can't help it. She has a soft spot for hard lovers.

Block touches his blockhead.

JULIA: She's more qualified than him, and he knows it. That's why he always keeps her beneath him. Now that she finally made it to the downtown office, he wants to get rid of her as competition. I hear they've already found someone to replace her.

BLOCK: Well I ...

Before Block can stop her, Julia knocks at the bedroom door.

ALLEN: (*to Evelyn*) Quick dear, in here!

He pushes her toward the closet.

EVELYN: We're married, Allen. We don't have to hide.

ALLEN: I'd almost forgotten. But just the same.

He jumps into the closet and pulls Evelyn in after him. Julia knocks again, then opens the door, looks in, sees no one, and closes it again. She leaves.

scene 7

Block paces about the room, then speaks to the audience.

BLOCK: Terrible story. Terrible thing for him to do. That's true. But what's it got to do with me, or you? Should I just quit? Put an end to it? Let all my work and plans be trumped by stupid chance? Sure, there's always someone who gets the short end of the log. Evelyn, the workers ... but come on ... would any of them stick up for me if I were the victim of some scheme? No, Block, stay focused. Let the others deal with hocus pocus. Remember: you've already won two hearts, and you can rise still higher! Is there some other heart out there, ready for an eager buyer?

Florian Moffat enters stage left and rings the doorbell. Block opens. Moffat is a squat old man. His tuxedo is too large for him by several sizes, and his black top hat is too small, tilting dangerously to the side of his head. Everything he wears is the purest white.

MOFFAT: Mr. Block, I don't believe we've met. I'm Florian Moffat, majority shareholder and chairman of the board of XYZ Group.

Block turns to the audience and shrugs.

BLOCK: (*turning back to Moffat*) Pleasure to meet you, sir. Have a seat, please. Have a drink.

MOFFAT: I'll only be a moment. I've been sent by the board on a fact-finding mission. Rumors have reached us to the effect that this company's executives have been engaged in immoral behavior.

BLOCK: That is what the workers have been saying.

MOFFAT: Oh, Lord no, not that kind of immorality. I mean immorality that matters. The seeds of our success are being wasted on frivolous carnal pursuits.

BLOCK: Carnal per– whats?

MOFFAT: –suits, Mr. Block.

BLOCK: I knew this suit was a waste.

MOFFAT: An anonymous informant, let's call him Hindman, has intimated that this very house has become a den of adultery.

BLOCK: Impossible! No one here has behaved anything like an adult.

MOFFAT: There's no need to fear for yourself, Mr. Block. I can see quite clearly that you present no threat of allurement to the softer sex, or the harder one.

BLOCK: Well I, thank you ...

MOFFAT: But perhaps they've taken advantage of their power over you and your house.

BLOCK: I couldn't rule out ...

MOFFAT: May I have a look around?

Before Block can answer, he heads straight to the bedroom. He looks under the covers, under the bed, behind the bed, behind the picture on the wall. Meanwhile. George enters stage left and rings the doorbell frantically, repeatedly, until Block finally goes to open the door.

GEORGE: (breathless) Block!

BLOCK: What is it?

GEORGE: The workers are on strike!

In the bedroom the closet door bursts open, and all its erstwhile inhabitants fall out, piling up on top of Florian Moffat. The curtain closes as the band plays "Solidarity Forever."

Act V.

Friday. At XYZ, Inc.

scene 1

When the curtain opens, we see the same set as in Act I. Only the column of portraits in the break room has changed. Florian Moffat is still at the top; beneath him now is Mr. Block; and beneath him, at the bottom of the column, is Rearman. The other bosses' portraits are gone. George is alone in the work room, working as pointlessly as the workers did in Act I, but more hurriedly and less effectively.

GEORGE: I'm sure they're on their way. Just a little late in starting off their day. Yesterday there was some tension, sure. Some misplaced thoughts, misspoken words. Rearman goes, "Work more, damn fools, work more!" And them ... they walked right out the door. But now we've had the night to cool our heads ... Oh, man, I wish someone else were foreman instead. (*He pauses, waiting for the others to arrive. Rearman enters, but George continues his monologue.*) I should have a talk with them. Come on, fellow workers, work! There are so many reasons to. There's ... well, there's ... and then, well, then, I know there are ... we just need to think this through ...

While George speaks, Rearman has been looking over the portraits on the wall, adjusting his until it's just right. Then he turns to George.

REARMAN: They aren't coming.

GEORGE: Give them time. (*The workers' chatter is heard offstage.*) See, there they are!

REARMAN: They aren't coming to work.

The workers—specifically Emma, Carla, and Don—begin to sing, still offstage.

THE WORKERS:

In our hands is placed a power greater than their hoarded gold,
Greater than the might of armies, magnified a thousand-fold ...

They enter stage left, carrying protest signs and still singing.

... solidarity forever, for the union makes us strong!

GEORGE: (*going to meet them outside*) Hey guys, I am so glad to see you here. I've put it all behind me, all of yesterday.

EMMA: George, let us talk to Block.

GEORGE: Block isn't boss here anymore. Florian Moffat demoted all the other execs and made Block CEO.

---

scene 2

Rearman goes outside to hang a big sign reading "LOCKOUT" above the entrance.

REARMAN: (*to the audience*) So far, so good. Just one more thing's still in my way. One thing "blocks" me, you could say. The others, high and mighty, they fell (*snaps his fingers*) just like that! But the final roadblock ... (*He looks up at Block's picture on the wall.*) Hey, what are you staring at?

Evelyn enters stage left and walks toward Rearman. The workers try to stop her from crossing the picket line, but she sneers at them and pushes her way through.

REARMAN: (*haughtily*) Ah, Evelyn, I am so glad you came. Come.

Rearman and Evelyn enter the building.

EVELYN: (*sullen*) What can I do for you?

REARMAN: What George is doing. George!

George resumes the work begun in Scene 1.

EVELYN: What's he doing?

REARMAN: Working. And make it count, eh? Push hard. Float the quotas. Venerate revenue. Negate negative growth. Keep your performance up, and we won't need the bums out there!

Evelyn doesn't react.

REARMAN: Well?

EVELYN: You want me to be a scab?

GEORGE: It's not a strike. There's just a misunderstanding. Anyway, the work's not so bad ...

He goes around again, doing the company's work. Evelyn looks on, horrified.

scene 3

Outside, the workers sing:

We shall not, we shall not be moved.
We shall not, we shall not be moved ...

Benedict arrives.

BENEDICT: How moving. You guys hardly move your asses even when you are working.

Clifford arrives.

CLIFFORD: Hey guys ... (*remembering*) oh, man, the strike! So I'm not late for work? Give me a sign!

CARLA: You were supposed to bring your own.

Clifford takes down the "LOCKOUT" sign, borrows a marker from Emma and amends it to read: "BLOCK/OUT!"

BENEDICT: Not working might suit you fine, but I'm going in.

CARLA: Benedict!

She tries to block his way, but he pushes past her and goes in. Victoria then enters stage left. She looks at the picket and hesitantly walks toward the workplace door.

CLIFFORD: (excited) We're on strike!

VICTORIA: You'll get us all fired.

CLIFFORD: Better fired than tired, I say. (*He bursts into song, to the tune of "Solidarity Forever."*)

Is there aught we hold in common with the suckers overworked
Who keep toiling every morning till they crack and go berserk?
No! For us the life of lounging is the one for which we work!
And—

VICTORIA: OK, OK, enough, just stop singing and give me a stupid sign.

Clifford gives her his sign. She takes it and holds it up, embarrassed. The band plays "Solidarity Forever."

---

scene 4

Block arrives.

THE WORKERS: (*turning to Block, speaking all at once*) Block, there's been a mistake! The bosses rejected our demands! Rearman's been misrepresenting you! Listen to us!

While they try to get Block's attention, Rearman runs out and pulls Block through the picket toward the door.

REARMAN: Pay no attention.

BLOCK: I make a point of paying nothing at all.

They enter the work room, where both George and Evelyn are busy at their tasks.

GEORGE: Block, thanks for coming. You need to sort this out. Things have gotten—

REARMAN: Just where we want them. We were handling them perfectly. Otherwise I would have called you myself. But it's good you came.

BLOCK: Good.

GEORGE: Say something to them. They'll listen to you.

REARMAN: Yes ... no, I have a better idea. Write a statement. A little sympathy (*for us*), a little passion (*contra them*). A clear, strong statement of the company's firm position.

BLOCK: Very firm.

REARMAN: But I know you're busy. You don't need to waste your time agonizing over the proper wording. Let me write it for you. You'll sign it. Or I'll sign it for you. Either way. But let's say the second way. Everything'll be fine.

BLOCK: Capital. (*He makes to leave, then sees Evelyn hard at work.*) Boss! I mean, Evelyn! I mean, what are you ... ?

She stops working.

EVELYN: I figured you'd feign ignorance.

BLOCK: Nothing comes to me more naturally.

EVELYN: I made you what you are, Block!

BLOCK: But really, what are you doing? Well now, whatever it is, keep it up!

EVELYN: I made you, and I can unmake you.

Block appears concerned, but before he can respond, Rearman escorts him out. The picketing workers accost him again.

BLOCK: (*to the workers*) I've already spoken with Rearman. He'll take care of everything.

Block leaves.

scene 5

In the work room, Evelyn stands up and makes to leave.

GEORGE: What are you doing?

EVELYN: What does it look like?

GEORGE: It looks like there's been another misunderstanding.

EVELYN: If that's what you want to call it. I can't believe anyone does this pointless work. What do you even make here?

Evelyn walks out. As the picketing workers watch her, Rearman pushes his way past them and enters the building. Seeing Evelyn leaving, he only shrugs.

REARMAN: Benedict, take over Evelyn's jobs.

BENEDICT: Why don't you take 'em?

Rearman's cell phone rings.

REARMAN: (*looking at the clock*) Ah, urgent business! Handle things, won't you?

He pats Benedict on the head and goes into the office, where he answers the phone and speaks too quietly for the audience to hear. Benedict shakes off the feeling of being patted on the head, then looks around and, seeing Rearman gone, also stops working.

GEORGE: What are you doing?

BENEDICT: Misunderstanding.

He leaves, walking past the picketers. He stops at the edge of the stage and sits down, watching from there. George goes back to work for a while. Then he stops, looks around, and reflects. Rearman, having finished his phone call, is typing on the office computer.

GEORGE: (*timidly*) Rearman? (*Rearman does not hear. George speaks more loudly.*) Rearman!

Still no reply. George sighs, stands up, and walks to the window. He sees Emma picketing. When she comes close to the window she notices him watching her and stops.

GEORGE: So, Emma ... does this mean you won't go out with me? There won't be anything between us?

EMMA: George, there's a wall that's between us.

Rearman enters the room holding up a piece of paper he's just printed.

REARMAN: Where'd Benedict go? (*George raises his palms to say he doesn't know. Rearman takes out his phone and makes a call. Into the phone he says:*) Yes, I'm beginning to have reservations about Block's managerial capabilities. He's driven away two of our best scabs.

Send reinforcements. (*He pauses, listening and smiling.*) Yes, everything is under control.

Rearman walks out to the picket line.

---

scene 6

The picketing workers hiss and shout at Rearman until he motions for them to let him speak.

REARMAN: You wanted to hear from Block?

He hands them the piece of paper he's been carrying. They gather around to read it.

CARLA: Block sent this?

REARMAN: Says your demands aren't worth the wood pulp you wrote them on.

DON: That's what he thinks of us?

REARMAN: And why not? Anyway, we've got a new batch of heroes already on the way. (*His cell phone beeps with sound of a new message. He looks at it and smiles.*) Here they are right now!

Allen Sacks, Ronald Dump, and Smelania Dump enter. Rearman hurries toward them and embraces them all.

REARMAN: (*cheerfully*) I was devastated when I heard! So shameful what they've done to you! Demoted! All for showing a little love—misplaced, perhaps, but what love isn't? There are some who love power and money, and they're blamed for not loving people. There are some who love people, and they're accused of disloyalty to power and money! But here you are. Reduced to this! And yet—what am I saying?—truly there's nothing more honorable. When our capital is wounded, who stops the bleeding? When the wound turns green with money, who covers over the festering? When the wheels of industry slow, who is there to get pulled into the gears? Reduced? No, you've been raised to this! To the only corporate title higher than CEO—without it, the CEOs would be nothing but beggars! Come, let us salute you, the elite of the base and the base of the elite—wear the badge with pride, O SCABS!

Heads held low, Allen, Ronald, and Smelania silently follow Rearman as he tries to push them through the picket line. For a while the workers keep them from crossing.

BENEDICT: Aw, just let 'em through. They won't last.

The picketers relent. The scabs enter the building, and Rearman quickly puts them to work with George. They begin working fast, pushing buttons, making calls, packing boxes. But soon their pace slows. Finally they stop working altogether. Only George keeps on, steadily. Rearman is in his office, typing again.

RONALD: (*wiping his brow*) I'm a tremendous worker. I could really get into this. How long have we been going?

GEORGE: (*looking at the clock*) A minute and a half.

RONALD: That was one excellent minute. The half wasn't bad either. I could easily do ten times this many. (*He goes back to work.*)

ALLEN: (*watching Ronald work, but still not working himself*) It doesn't demand half the industriousness that the workers let on. (*He looks at the clock.*)

Ronald stops working again.

RONALD: (*wiping his brow again*) This is why I understand working people. Look at those lazy losers outside. Here inside, this is where the real workers are! Right, Smelania? (*She glares at him.*) Aw, don't be such a sourpuss. Come here, my little pussycat.

He grabs her and tries to kiss her. She pulls herself free and walks toward the door.

SMELANIA: I have an appointment.

ALLEN: With whom?

SMELANIA: Anyone but you two.

She leaves.

RONALD: Who needs her? We've got each other. I love it here.

ALLEN: (*standing up*) My, look at the time! I entirely forgot my ... indeed, yes ... I'm confident you can handle it, Ronald. I happily leave it in your hands. (*leaving*) Smelania! Wait!

RONALD: Who needs him? (*He goes back to work, very intensely, for a few seconds. Then he stops.*) I wish I could stay here all day. If only I weren't so popular. They want me to go star in another play. Better than this one. I was holding out as long as I could, but I have to give the people what they want. You'll be all right here, won't you, mister?

Ronald pats George on the back, then leaves. Outside, Emma has stopped picketing and watches George through the window. Rearman enters the work room, looks around and, grinning, shakes his head. Holding a new piece of paper, he leaves the building, walks past the picket, and exits the stage. George keeps working for a little longer. Then he stops and, considering that he's the only one left working for this company, throws his tools angrily to the ground. He walks outside to join the picket. Emma joins him and gives him her sign.

---

scene 7

Rearman enters stage left with Florian Moffat. They stop before the picket line.

REARMAN: I apologize, Mr. Moffat, for bringing you all the way out here. But I felt you should see it for yourself.

MOFFAT: Yes, I see. What is this, a picnic?

REARMAN: No sir, a *picket*. Our workers are on strike.

MOFFAT: My workers. Very interesting.

REARMAN: This is terrible for our company.

MOFFAT: My company.

REARMAN: Quite. Mr. Moffat, a strike is the most dangerous thing in the world.

MOFFAT: My world.

REARMAN: Indeed. It should be crushed in its infancy, aborted before birth, erased from our thoughts before it could even be conceived.

MOFFAT: Abstinence is the only ethical option.

REARMAN: Yet here it is. Conceived, born, and thriving. There is one clear explanation: CEO Block does not want to break the strike.

MOFFAT: Impossible.

REARMAN: He has been driving away all our scabs. And then, most recently he wrote this letter for me to deliver to the workers. I hope you'll understand if I betrayed his trust for the sake of yours. I opened it and read it.

He gives Moffat the piece of paper he has been holding. Moffat reads it and frowns.

MOFFAT: "Dump the bosses"? "People before Moffats"? I find it hard to believe that Mr. Block ...

REARMAN: I was as shocked as you. And yet there is sense to it. Not so long ago he was one of them. He is still close to them. He hasn't yet managed to forget where he came from.

MOFFAT: But you have.

REARMAN: There's more. I also have reason to question Block's moral fortitude. He has been engaged in an inappropriate relationship with Julia Sacks, who is his subordinate in the company, and who is, moreover, much too charming and intelligent for him.

MOFFAT: I will take this into consideration.

Evelyn enters, stage left.

EVELYN: Mr. Moffat, I've been looking for you.

MOFFAT: Yes?

EVELYN: It's about Block.

MOFFAT: About his morality?

EVELYN: He's been unfaithful to my daughter Julia.

MOFFAT: Unfaithful, my word.

EVELYN: My word, actually.

MOFFAT: But how do you know?

EVELYN: He tried to seduce me.

MOFFAT: With success?

REARMAN: We can't have an immoral CEO.

EVELYN: Is there any other kind?

MOFFAT: This is serious indeed. You've persuaded me, Mr. Rearman. (*He shakes Rearman's hand.*) CEO Rearman.

REARMAN: I can't thank you enough. (*Pause*) No, I think that was enough. (*pause*) I have just one small request.

MOFFAT: Yes?

REARMAN: Give Julia Sacks a position in my office.

MOFFAT: I would love to, but ... considering the threats to her morality that appear to lurk on all sides, and (*growing excited*) considering the exceptional characteristics in her which may arouse dangerous impulses in those susceptible to them (*more excited*), in order to protect this flower (*still more excited*) of XYZ Group from the lascivious world ... (*calming down*) I have decided to make her my own personal secretary. Fear not. I shall never, ever, let her out of my sight.

He tips his small hat, elegantly catches it as it falls off his head, and leaves. Evelyn follows, scowling.

---

scene 8

REARMAN: (*still standing before the picket line, speaking to the audience*) The company's in my hands, and I'll throw the strikers onto the streets. If only Julia were here with me, my happiness would be complete.

Julia enters, stage left.

REARMAN: Julia!

JULIA: I'm looking for Block.

REARMAN: Mr. Block is presently at the downtown office. But he won't be there for long. Here, come wait inside.

JULIA: No.

REARMAN: Right, don't wait for that blockhead.

JULIA: I heard about him and my mom. He cheats the workers, then me, then her—is there anyone he hasn't cheated yet?

REARMAN: Me. But come on, Block is too stupid to really cheat anyone. He still can't even figure out which side he's on. What do you want with him anyway?

JULIA: I wanted to finally ask him which side he's on.

REARMAN: Ah, Julia, your silly questions ... You know, I was about to head downtown myself. Come with me. If we work together, just think where we could go.

JULIA: I know exactly where you can go.

Rearman storms off. The band plays "Which Side Are You On?" and Julia joins the picketing workers as they sing along.

---

scene 9

A phone rings inside the workplace. The picketers stop and listen. George steps toward the door, then stops.

CLIFFORD: Don't pick up. We're on strike.

GEORGE: It could be them asking to negotiate.

The phone rings again. George goes inside and picks up.

GEORGE: (*into the phone*) Yes, yes, I understand. Can you hold?

He walks back outside, slowly, with an expression of fear.

EMMA: Who was it?

CARLA: What did they want?

GEORGE: It's the National Guard. They've been called in to put down the strike. By any means necessary. (He pauses.) They're asking for directions.

The workers are silent for some time, until Block enters, stage left.

BLOCK: Hey ho, associates, why the round faces? You look more lost than the National Guard I ran into when I was vacating the corporate offices. Armed to the teeth they were, but Boss bless 'em, poor fellas couldn't tell the butt of their rifles from the butt of a joke or a joke about butts. Had to ask me the way to the picket line.

EMMA: Block! Did you tell them?

The workers look on in fearful anticipation. Before Block answers, Florian Moffat hobbles on stage, waving his arms. Rearman hangs behind him.

---

scene 10

MOFFAT: A moment, a moment, dear fellows and ladies. I have a very important announcement. As you know, XYZ Group has shown extraordinary growth during the last quarter (of an hour), and you will be especially interested to learn of our latest acquisition. You see ... (*motions to the band*) ... appropriate music, please ... (*the band plays dramatic music*) ... you see, XYZ Group is expanding ... into the theater business! It has purchased this very theater! (*The workers look on in silence.*) And the play is over.

EMMA: What?

MOFFAT: Terribly sorry, but the board of XYZ was growing concerned for you. Your work ethic was becoming dangerously unethical. It was imperative to nip it in the butt.

EMMA: Bud.

MOFFAT: Indeed, bud is also unethical.

CARLA: But how was the play going to end?

MOFFAT: Naturally, Mr. Block was facing a tragic fall from power. No need to see that through.

VICTORIA: I knew it. You never let anyone but yourselves make it to the top.

MOFFAT: He began to show insufficient love for his superiors. As they say, the meek may inherit the dirt, but the rich will inherit the skyscrapers.

CARLA: His mistake was to turn against us! You stopped the play just when he was about to realize we could all make it to the top if we stuck together!

JULIA: Block, did you turn against the company? I knew you would!

DON: Maybe he showed his love for Rearman and Moffat by ordering them an exploding Valentine. Or a pie in the sky.

BLOCK: Well I ...

EMMA: But what did Block do about the National Guard and the strike? What were we going to find out?

MOFFAT: That's none of your concern now. Julia, come along, dear. Your office awaits you. My office, that is.

Moffat waits. Julia doesn't move.

JULIA: I bet Block gave the National Guard directions to jump right into the lake.

CLIFFORD: You know what I think. He probably sent 'em straight to corporate headquarters with instructions to bash in anything they find.

MOFFAT: (*suddenly worried*) Mr. Block, is that possible?

BLOCK: Well sir, I respect our disservice men and women! Would it be right to invite them to a rundown place like we have out here, when they could be kicking up their boots on leather couches and resting their bayonets against glass windows downtown?

MOFFAT: Mr. Rearman, have you spoken with anyone from headquarters?

REARMAN: I'll be right on it.

He rushes off, phone in hand.

EMMA: But what about the other plotlines?

JULIA: Did my mom find a better place to work?

GEORGE: Was Emma finally going to out with me?

DON: And Cliff with Vicky? And everyone with me?

BENEDICT: Please, any ending but that!

MOFFAT: Lights! (*The spotlights go off and non-theatrical lighting goes on.*)

Aggie comes on stage, dressed again as Joe Hill, carrying a broom. She sweeps at Moffat until she sweeps him right off the stage. When Moffat's gone, she turns to the workers.

AGGIE: Hey, you know what? You can have any ending you want. Does Block stop being a blockhead, or does he just keep on trying to make it to the top without the rest of you? It depends on you. Because it's not just about that guy over here. It's about all the Misters Block out there. Yes, you saw it. Mr. Block has a tragic flow: the belief that workers can succeed in the wage system without solidarity. This is his personal flaw, and as long as it's a part of him—as long as he thinks he's just himself, and not one of you—then it keeps bringing him down. But this isn't just his flaw. Is there any flaw in the world more widely shared? And yet: when Block displays his tragic flaw up here on stage, he lets us all see it, laugh at it, and turn his tragedy into our comedy. His failure can be our victory. But this is what I mean: it lets all of us Misters Block laugh our own selves and realize it's about time for us to stop being Block. And that's where love comes in. Love upsets the tragic balance. If we're just in love with the bosses, then Block's tragedy turns into our shared farce. But if we love one another, then we'll stop being blockheads! But that's where the play the ends. Nothing more to see up here onstage. The rest is up to you to act out in the world!

The curtain does not close as the actors and audience merge and disperse, while the band plays "Mr. Block."

Postscript

The following text is printed on the version of the program handed out at the end of the Intermission, before Act IV:

When we look at Mr. Block's position from the perspective of his personal success, his position is tragic, because he is destined to fail. The only way out would be to stop being a blockhead. From the perspective of the working class as a whole, however, Mr. Block's destiny is comic. The class can take pleasure in watching Block try and fail, because his fall shows the way to the class's rise. The class struggle is played out in the conflict between comedy's Thalia and tragedy's Melpomene. And as Thalia's constant companion on stage is Eros, love enters, leading everywhere and nowhere. The working class in love can overcome its tragic existence and laugh at its conditions. But the employing class in love with itself, and workers in love with their employers, only make fools of themselves. Before giving way to offstage epic, their tragicomedy unmakes itself as farce.

Yes, as someone once said, all great events happen twice, first as tragedy and then as farce. Small events happen twice as well, but simultaneously. Which event you see depends on how you look, and where you stand.

Advance Praise for *Praise Boss!*

In Joe Grim Feinberg's pun-packed, risqué play, Mr. Block acts on one universal truth: That work is the worst way to make a buck. But rather than standing in solidarity with his coworkers, Mr. Block schemes and puts the "organ" in organizing his way to the top!

— Jason Krpan, former chair of the Industrial Workers of the World

Joe Grim Feinberg's "proletarian sex tragicomedy" is extraordinary. But it also accomplishes something extraordinarily rare in the theatre of our moment. *Praise Boss!* boldly reclaims key characters and dynamics of labor battles past and vividly reimagines them for a contemporary moment of fractious capitalism that is at once late and all too soon.

— Richard Byrne, playwright, editor, journalist

Praise Boss! is Joe Feinberg's mad mix of vaudeville, IWW history, cartoon, Agit Prop, erotic high jinks, and class struggle. Here's a play on almost everything—with the Revolution in mind. It's a natural for radio, film, or video—i.e., pure radical theatre. Not for the faint of heart—*Praise Boss!* delivers some solid punches—with a very strong Left Hand.

— Warren Leming, author, poet, Kerr devotee

Praise Boss! cannot be more timely! Mr. Block, that exploited worker who loves his exploiters, is not just a laughable character unaware of his own best class interest. It is you and me, most of the time. We just have good excuses. Its author Joseph Grim Feinberg is a rare species. You do not often meet a meticulous scholar, a wandering international intellectual, a fine critical theorist, and a genuine humorist in one person. In the times of political despair when indeed all our heroes are dead and our enemies are in power, his resurrection of Brechtian theatre in its best tradition is at the same time a literary feast and a call for action.

— Igor Štiks, the author of *The Judgement of Richard Richter* and *W: A Novel*

Joseph Grim Feinberg's *Praise Boss* concerns the further adventures of a very old character, one who sadly seems more of the current moment than ever before. Self-serving and self-delusional Mr. Block fits perfectly into a world dominated by false narratives, whether put forth by demagogues, social media, or some combination of the two. That he seems to thrive in this world suggests how far we've all strayed from the goals of dignity, equality, and equity the IWW champions. But Feinberg's play suggests that most stories don't end where we think and that the power to change the outcome has always rested with us.

— Paul Durica, Newberry Library

Thanks

Mr. Block would never have made it out of the workplaces of the world and onto my imagined stage without the inspiration of Penelope and Franklin Rosemont, who introduced me to the fellow and his storied life. It was Jason Krpan, then, who helped me realize how much Block there is in all of us—and how laughing at him helps us get him out. It was in conversation with Fellow Worker Krpan that many of the characters in the play came to life, the scenes took shape, and the worst of the jokes were scuttled. (Yes, the first draft contained even worse jokes than those you'll find here.) No less gratitude is due to my readers and critics from the Globe Café in Prague, especially Danielle Bodnar, Jindra Čekan, Shelby Glynn, Daniel Lamken, Zoheb Mashiur, and Mark Stroup. And thanks to Tamara Smith for giving Mr. Block the chance to come back to the Charles H. Kerr Publishing Co., truly the best company he ever kept.